Living with stress
and promoting well-being

A HANDBOOK FOR NURSES

Edited by

KAREN E. CLAUS, Ph.D.
Co-director, Stress Management Project,
and Assistant Research Psychologist,
University of California School of Nursing,
San Francisco, California

JUNE T. BAILEY,
R.N., Ed.D., F.A.A.N.
Director, Stress Management Project,
and Professor and Associate Dean,
University of California School of Nursing,
San Francisco, California

The C. V. Mosby Company

ST. LOUIS • TORONTO • LONDON   1980

Copyright © 1980 by The C. V. Mosby Company

All rights reserved. No part of this book may be reproduced in any manner without written permission of the publisher.

Printed in the United States of America

The C. V. Mosby Company
11830 Westline Industrial Drive, St. Louis, Missouri 63141

Library of Congress Cataloging in Publication Data

Main entry under title:

Living with stress and promoting well-being.

  Bibliography: p.
  Includes index.
    1. Nursing—Psychological aspects. 2. Job stress.
3. Intensive care nursing—Psychological aspects. I.
Claus, Karen E. II. Bailey, June T. [DNLM: 1. Stress,
Psychological—Nursing texts. WY87 L785]
RT86.L58   610.73'0692   80-14605
ISBN 0-8016-1148-2

C/M/M 9 8 7 6 5 4 3 2   02/C/252

Contributors

PAMELA BAJ, R.N., M.S.

Formerly Research Assistant, University of California School of Nursing, San Francisco; Instructor, University of San Francisco, San Francisco, California

ANN BALDWIN, R.N., Ph.D.

Assistant Research Nurse, University of California School of Nursing, San Francisco, California

JAMES W. GROUT, M.A.

Research Specialist, University of California School of Nursing, San Francisco, California

JAN MacLACHLAN, R.N., B.S.

Staff Nurse, Stanford University Hospital, Palo Alto, California

JUDITH ANN MORAN, R.N., M.S.

Doctoral Student, DNS Program, and Research Assistant, University of California School of Nursing, San Francisco, California

HANS SELYE, C.C., M.D., Ph.D., D.Sc.

President, International Institute of Stress, University of Montreal, Montreal, Quebec, Canada

SUSAN M. STEFFEN, R.N., M.S.

Lecturer, University of California School of Nursing, San Francisco, California

MARGRETTA M. STYLES, R.N., Ed.D., F.A.A.N.

Professor and Dean, University of California School of Nursing, San Francisco, California

PATTY ZINDLER-WERNET, R.N., M.S.

Lecturer, University of California School of Nursing, San Francisco, California

Preface

Few of us would dispute the notion that stress pervades our society or that it has a profound effect on our daily living. Ours is an age of change, uncertainty, technocracy, and ever-increasing demands. Indeed, the excessive demands placed on us are often deleterious to our well-being and to our feelings of productivity and fulfillment.

The concept of stress is complex, multifaceted, and a frequently misunderstood phenomenon. Much of what we know about stress has come about through the tireless efforts and fifty years of research by an internationally renowned scientist, Dr. Hans Selye, known as "the Father of the Stress Concept," for whom we have the utmost respect.

Although we will be presenting major concepts of Dr. Selye's work relative to biological stress, our approach to stress is psychological in nature, primarily because of our training, experience, professional roles, and interest.

Our interest in studying stress derives essentially from graduate students enrolled in a program of study with us that prepared them for leadership roles in a variety of health care and educational settings. Over the years we noted that approximately half of our students, who had previously worked in critical care nursing units, had opted to return to the university to prepare themselves for a different role. Many of our students indicated that they left ICU nursing because they felt they could no longer cope effectively with the stress they encountered on the job.

After almost a decade of working with students, conducting some preliminary investigations, and more recently enlarging our study of job-related stress in nursing, we now wish to share with the reader our perspectives on stress and some of the results of our study on the perception of stress of approximately 1800 ICU nurses. In essence, this book is not only written *about* nurses, but perhaps more importantly it is written *for* nurses.

In addition, the book is designed to (1) increase the reader's understanding of the nature of stress through presentation of a conceptual model of stress-management processes, (2) present strategies whereby management can deal more effectively with job-related stress, (3) offer individuals ways to increase their awareness of stressors, evaluate their response, and cope in ways that will maximize their well-being, and (4) adapt more effectively to both positive and negative stresses in their daily living.

We recognize that the real value of *Living With Stress and Promoting Well-Being* rests with the individual. It is our hope that this book will challenge nurses to experiment with various modalities of stress-reduction techniques, determine what works best for them, practice the art of reducing stress, and most of all, harness the positive energy of stress to improve their own well-being and the well-being of their patients.

This book was made possible by the award of a special training project grant* to the School of Nursing, University of California, San Francisco. We gratefully acknowledge the Public Health Service and the University of California for the opportunity to implement the goals of the project.

In addition, we also wish to thank Stanford University for permitting us to use their facilities and resources in order to implement and evaluate a "Stress Reduction Training Program for Intensive Care Nurses."† A special "thank you" is extended to Duane Walker, Associate Administrator, Hospitals and Clinics/Director of Nursing Service, Stanford University Hospital, and to Nancy Madsen, Associate Director, Nursing Service. Through their encouragement and management actions, we were able to implement and evaluate the Stress Reduction Training Program for Stanford Intensive Care Nurses.

Our warmest appreciation is expressed and extended to all nursing service directors throughout the region who facilitated our stress survey, to officers of the American Association of Critical Care Nurses who provided the impetus for the Regional Stress Audit, and to the 1800 nurses who participated in the stress survey. Without the interest and support of these nurses, the project would not have attained one of its major goals.

Rebecca Partridge, a member of the Stress Management Project staff during the early years of the project, deserves special recognition. Miss Partridge contributed to the development of the Stress Questionnaire and assisted in the data collection and the analysis of the data. We also wish to thank Brigid Doyle and Jane Binger for their assistance in the data analysis.

---

*"Stress Reduction Training Program for Intensive Care Nurses," special training project grant D10 NU02072, Division of Nurses, Health Resources Administration.
†The results of the Stress Reduction Training Program will be reported later in a series of articles.

The invaluable assistance of members of the project staff and their contributions were indeed vital in making this book a reality. To each of them, and to our other contributors, we offer our sincere thanks.

We wish to express our special indebtedness to Dr. Margretta Styles, Dean and Professor, University of California School of Nursing, San Francisco, for her review of the manuscript and for her provocative chapter on what lies ahead for nurses in the next decade. Dr. Hans Selye, an internationally known scientist, graciously consented to share with the reader his philosophical views and insights on stress in the concluding chapter. We applaud and thank him for his interest in nursing.

Our warmest appreciation is extended to Beth Graham and to Anne Ossulston for their tireless efforts and assistance in transcribing numerous tapes, typing a multitude of drafts, and for their technical assistance. We are particularly grateful to Dianne Hendricks, a member of the School of Nursing faculty, who assisted us in the final editing of the manuscript.

In conclusion, we wish to express our indebtedness to members of our families who many times found us "in absentia," both in mind and in body. For their continued understanding and caring, we extend our love and appreciation.

Karen E. Claus
June T. Bailey

Contents

2|

PART ONE

The nurse and stress

CHAPTER 1

Change and challenge in nursing— the road ahead

Margretta M. Styles

Stresses on a profession create stresses on its members. The converse is also true.

Nursing, with a big N, is the environment to which the nurse was attracted, within which she was indoctrinated, within which she practices, and which she determines. Nursing and the nurse are mutual influences. Therefore an understanding of the stressors and adaptive behaviors of one is important to an understanding of the stressors and adaptive behaviors of the other. This chapter is intended to provide, in brief, a current and future perspective on the nursing profession at large and thus to serve as a framework through which to view the nurse at work.

The state of nursing today can be best explained, and the road ahead charted, by giving proper cognizance to three dominant factors that place enormous demands on the system:

1. Nursing is an occupation in the throes of professionalization.
2. Nursing is almost exclusively practiced within an institutional context.
3. Nursing is largely an occupation of women.

THE PROFESSIONALIZATION OF NURSING

Professionalization is not so much a discrete state that an occupation achieves as a tendency manifested by some occupations more than others. A number of characteristics are associated with this tendency. The vocations commonly identified as being most professional comprise those which control both admission to the field and the ethical and scientific standards of practice and which are accorded special privilege by society.

Occupations engaged in professionalization, the process whereby this tendency is developed, traditionally employ a number of means to pursue their goal. They align themselves with universities, within which they assert themselves as scholarly disciplines as well as fields of public service. In the academic setting, educational programs for the professions are formalized, extended, and specialized, and research of a pure and applied nature is conducted. In professionalizing, occupations also develop credentialing systems as principal instruments of control and self-governance. Although established with the avowed and often real intent of protecting various publics through quality assurance, these credentialing mechanisms also serve as gatekeepers, regulating access to the field. Accreditation promotes the rights of institutions to engage in education and service, and licensing and certification promote the rights of individuals to engage in general and specialty practice.

A popular theory exists that change occurs in organizations in a cyclical fashion, moving through stages of evolution, crisis, and revolution (Lippitt & Schmidt, 1967). Viewed from this proposition, nursing can be seen as having proceeded heretofore in an evolutionary manner with respect to the educational and credentialing trends associated with professionalization. Nursing stands now at a critical juncture, which realistically could be construed as the crisis in the change cycle, precipitated by the organized effort of the profession to persuade its members and various consumers of the necessity for upgrading to the baccalaureate level the educational requirements for entry into professional practice (American Nurses' Association, 1978). Corollaries to this movement are the equally determined efforts of a number of states to break from the current national pattern of RN licensure and enact differentiated licensing, reflecting the educational requirement proposed for professional practice.

Moreover, the credentialing system is also in a crisis of competition and lack of coordination, resulting in proliferation, duplication, and fragmentation of these mechanisms and the transmission of unclear, weak signals and undue costs to the public. Recognition of the critical nature of these problems prompted *the Study of Credentialing in Nursing,* which in a January, 1979, report recommended future directions for the profession to move from crisis to systematic change or, as may be seen, through revolution again to evolution (National Committee for the Study of Credentialing in Nursing, 1979).

These credentialing problems and the proposed solutions, which have the profession in spasm, are also cataclysmic events for the individual nurse who, in facing an uncertain future, weighs in the balance her needs versus those of a metamorphic profession and the society to be served. It is not an exaggeration to refer to the state in which a nurse thus finds herself as that of an "identity crisis," since one of the major functions of a credentialing system is to provide occupational identity and role delineation for the credentialed individual. A change in the system is inevitably and understandably perceived as a threat to the person whose very definition of role is dependent on that system. The underlying themes of this concern are, "Will I be left behind? Will I somehow be depreciated as the profession moves ahead?" and, "At what expense can I stay abreast of these developments?" Specific issues within these themes relate to the grandfathering (i.e., exempting from prohibitive legislation those already engaged in an activity before the legislation was passed) of nurses as new licensing and certifying systems are established, as avenues for educational mobility become available, as practice and credentialing demands are increased, and as requirements for relicensure and recertification are established to assure that competence is maintained.

INSTITUTIONAL CONTEXT FOR NURSING PRACTICE

Nursing's efforts to professionalize have been frustrated by the tradition of its operation within an organizational setting; whereas, with many of the earliest and best established professions such as medicine, dentistry, and law, it is the common mode that practitioners work independently and directly with their clients. In the institutions in which nursing is generally practiced, an employer and a second value system are interposed between the nurse and the patient. This militates against gaining control over standards of practice, a hallmark of professionalism, unless extremely specific arrangements have been made to guarantee these rights and responsibilities. In recent times the nursing profession has intensified its pressures and inventiveness in developing these arrangements.

Nurses thereby find themselves torn between the powerful cross-currents of the institution and the profession. They are literally the pivotal point of the battle for nursing's self-determinism, a struggle complicated by the variable understanding and conviction of nurses who have joined in the fray.

Chief among the measures whereby the nursing profession seeks to strengthen control of its practice in institutions are collective bargaining, innovative staffing patterns, and organizational designs.

In serving as bargaining agents for their members in those institutions where contracts have been negotiated, state nurses' associations have been vociferous in their support of raising standards of nursing as well as the economic and general welfare of the nurse. It would require a survey of individual contracts and their consequences to determine the relative attention paid to these two purposes. However, there is no question as to the serious wedge often driven between staff nurses and nurse administrators and between nurse administrators and their professional association as a result of this union activity. Collective bargaining, as a device for promoting the goals of professionalization, has emerged as a double-edged sword.

Primary nursing, all registered nurse staffs, and clinical and specialist series are examples of efforts (1) to simplify the cluttered staffing patterns and refocus the diffuse accountability that accompanied the proliferation of ancillary nursing personnel after the acute shortage period of World War II; (2) to recognize the authority and effect of expertise; (3) to raise standards of care; and (4) to sharpen the blurred image and the flabby negotiating posture that occurs when nursing is delivered by myriad workers at the bedside. The growth of intensive care units, in which there is neither margin for ineptitude nor time for supervision, may well have stimulated or given credence and strength to these movements.

As nurses have become more daring, economically sophisticated, and enterprising, radical organizational readjustments have been propounded. The concepts of professional nursing staffs with defined privileges and of professional corporations providing complete or selected nursing services to institutions by contract are being developed. Such arrangements challenge nurses, finally and fully ensconced at the professional controls, to set appropriate standards and goals and to provide high-quality care in a cost-effective manner.

Health care agencies, on the other hand, have made strong bids to exert their governance over the professional nurse. The most obvious of these attempts is advocacy of institutional licensure, a proposal for which there has been flickering and weakening support. Such a system would place all credentialing within the hands of the employer, who would literally have a stranglehold over the nurse. Professional identity and mobility would be a concept and a privilege of the past. Talk of institutional licensure has served a constructive purpose for nursing, since it is one issue that unites and inflames nurses in opposition.

Many nurses on the job witness and experience myriad and diverse institutional efforts, whose goal or effect is that of "dividing to conquer" the nursing body and eroding its professional authority within the system. Some, a minority, are privileged to design and participate in structural changes in institutions that recognize and strengthen the rights and responsibilities associated with professional expertise.

NURSING AS A FIELD FOR WOMEN

The facts point out irrefutably that nursing is now predominantly an occupation for women and will be for some time to come (American Nurses' Association, 1977). It is more difficult to document the specific effects on the development of the field that can be attributed to this circumstance. However, few would doubt that this is a significant factor in the professionalization of nursing. There are sex linkages to the problems of control, economics, and status.

Women, as individuals, experience discrimination in our society. This discrimination and its consequences are magnified in a women's collective, such as nursing. Many of these problems are within the internal environment of the field. They reflect the socialization of women and the resultant lack of self-esteem, assertiveness, and group cohesion needed for strong individual and collective action and for effective collaborative relationships with other health professionals.

In examining nursing's external environment, although it is difficult to demonstrate cause and effect related to gender in the nursing profession, obvious discrepancies can be noted. Nursing has followed, and even led, some of the other occupations in the educational and credentialing trends associated with professionalization. For decades nursing education has been offered at the highest level possible, that of the doctorate. Nurses engage in research of improving quality and quantity. Licensing and accreditation systems in nursing have served as models for other fields. Yet, as mentioned earlier, the control of practice has not ensued to the degree that might be expected. In addition, the economic rewards are well below those of other professions. Nursing salary differentials, recognizing advanced preparation, are disappointing. Data collected for *The Study of Credentialing in Nursing* (National Committee for the Study of Credentialing in Nursing, 1979) indicate that nurses certified for specialty practice have made little financial gain, whereas specialists in other fields, such as medicine, find their income considerably increased and sometimes multiplied over former levels.

Nurses may find that the greatest and most telling blow of all is that their services generally receive meager recognition on the catalog of hospital costs to the patient. Nursing care, ranging from that provided by an aide to that of a highly educated clinical expert, is not separately identified but is lumped together under room and board on the list of charges. Third party reimbursement for nursing service, now in its infancy, and initiatives in isolated institutions will crack this barrier to nursing's advancement to professionhood.

SUMMARY

This chapter has surveyed some of the forces in the larger environment of the nursing profession that are a major influence on the nurse at work. These stressors are seen as relating to nursing's efforts toward professionalization, the institutional setting for nursing, and nursing as a woman's field.

". . . The Road Ahead," for the nurse as well as the profession, depends on the ability of those in the profession to recognize and make constructive use of these social, political, educational, credentialing, and economic factors in charting the future.

REFERENCES

American Nurses' Association. *Facts about nursing* 76-77. Kansas City: American Nurses' Association Publications, 1977.

American Nurses' Association. Resolutions. *The American Nurse,* September 15, 1978, *10*(9), 9-10.

Lippitt, G., & Schmidt, W. Crises in a developing organization. *Harvard Business Review,* 1967, *45*(6), 102-112.

National Committee for the Study of Credentialing in Nursing. *The study of credentialing in nursing: A new approach* (Vol. 1). *The report of the committee.* Kansas City: American Nurses' Association Publications, 1979.

SUGGESTED READINGS

Hershey, N. Institutional licensure for health professionals? *Hospital Progress,* 1976, *57,* 76-80; 124.

Hershey, N. Alternative to mandatory licensure of health professionals. *Hospital Progress,* 1969, *50,* 72-75.

Kelly, L. Institutional licensure. *Nursing Outlook,* 1973, *21,* 566-572.

Levine, L. Institutional licensure versus individual licensure. *Journal of Allied Health,* 1978, *7,* 109-114.

CHAPTER 2

The nature of stress

Karen E. Claus

Stress, and its effect on the health status of individuals, health care providers, and other occupational groups, has become a problem of national concern. Since Selye began his work on the nature of stress in the early 1930s, the problem has captured the attention of a wide variety of disciplines—physiology, psychology, sociology, medicine, and others. In the last decade interest has increased considerably, but the approaches to the study of stress are varied and sometimes confusing.

DEFINING STRESS

Among investigators there is little agreement on a universal definition of stress; nor is there agreement on a classification system for types of stress. The way in which stress is conceptualized depends largely on the investigator's interest and field of study.

Another problem is that none of the present concepts adequately explains how psychosocial stressors stimulate physiological reactions in the body. The unresolved question is: "How do environmental stimuli excite or induce bodily reactions that are harmful to health?" Within each conceptual framework there seems to be a missing link. Frequently the link concerns the perceptual or intellectual processes that a person applies to incoming stimuli in determining whether or not the stimuli are harmful. In other words, before environmental demands become stress, some intermediary mechanism is necessary to interpret what is going on. This intermediary mechanism may be the element that excites the body.

The confusion in the literature on the definition of stress and the disagreement among eminent researchers who have studied the concept of stress for years create a problem for those who want to develop a viable stress management training program. Identification of behaviors that are to be encouraged or reinforced through instruction and practice appears to be essential. Teaching cannot occur unless concepts can be clearly defined. Therefore a thorough review of the stress literature was conducted and is presented in Chapter 5.

Definition of stress

Stress is conceptualized as a universal phenomenon in which the individual *perceives* environmental stimuli as taxing the physiological, psychological, or sociological systems, whereby responses can be adaptive or maladaptive. The definition is supported in some degree by the work of two eminent stress researchers. We have borrowed heavily on the work of Dr. Hans Selye, the father of the "stress concept," and on the work of Dr. Richard Lazarus, who has been concerned with the psychological aspects of stress. Selye has defined stress in physiological terms as "the nonspecific response of the body to any demands made upon it" (Selye, 1975, p. 14). Lazarus has defined stress as environmental or internal demands that tax or exceed the adaptive resources of a system (Lazarus, 1971).

Both Selye and Lazarus emphasize the importance of perception in determining whether or not a stressor is negative or positive. Perception is a psychological phenomenon. It involves receiving information and the cognitive appraisal of that information. In cognitive appraisal, phenomena are categorized as to their positive or negative effects on human beings. Uncertainty about the nature of a stimulus encourages arousal of the protective physiological mechanisms of the body. Individuals react as if they were under threat. This may or may not, in reality, be justifiable. If individuals react to a stimulus as if it is threatening and, in actuality, it is not, then mentally they must retain their cognitive consistency by rationalizing their defensive behavior (Festinger, 1957; Heider, 1958). Sometimes this behavior leads to long chains of rationalization and overt actions that culminate in true psychological and physiological depletion.

Perception is the key

One of the most confusing aspects of the stress concept is determining whether stress is a stimulus or a response, or whether it is an interaction between the two. Selye has attempted to clarify the issue by indicating that, since any demand placed on the body is stress, individuals must then differentiate between positive and negative stressors through their perceptual processes. Lazarus has preferred to limit the term "stress" to only those demands which tax the system and require some additional energy input to maintain a steady state. Both Selye and Lazarus indicate that a system uses up some of its limited resources or "adaptation energy" when it responds to a perceived stressor. Energy expended in coping with one stressor may render the system vulnerable to other stressors.

Perception is the key to what Selye calls the internal and external conditioning factors, which determine how a stimulus is judged by an organism. Perception also determines how the physiological systems react to a stimulus input.

Perception is a cognitive process and, as such, is amenable to educational use. Training professionals how to manage stress in the environment is largely cognitively oriented. People can be taught to become aware of those stimuli which trigger defensive reactions and to develop coping strategies.

Two persons working side by side often perceive the same stimulus differently. One may see it as a stressor, whereas the other may see it as a challenge. Our research has indicated that the fast pace and crisis level of operation in intensive care units induce different perceptions, reactions, and responses in different nurses. Some nurses report the "high" they derive from the constant state of alertness and heavy performance demands, whereas others report the feeling of physical exhaustion and mental depletion. If perception makes the difference, it is possible to train people to be aware of how they view and react to stimuli.

MODEL OF STRESS MANAGEMENT

Our earlier work with systems models (Bailey & Claus, 1975; Claus & Bailey, 1977) has given us an appreciation of the applicability of cybernetics to everyday life. We have been particularly concerned with developing models that would help us effectively teach concepts of management and administration to graduate health care professionals. Our interest in developing stress management training programs for health professionals derived from the fact that a large percentage of our graduate students indicated that they had left high-paying positions as intensive care nurses because of stress. Our association with health professionals has led us to believe that stress is a major occupational hazard for well-trained persons who are engaged in human services such as the delivery of health care.

Psychological model

Perception. The model we present here is a psychological model with a focus on perception. We believe that perception is the key to determining whether or not environmental stimuli are going to induce defense mechanisms and resistance in an individual. Perception is an intellectual process involving information processing at physiological levels as well as at high levels of abstraction, such as categorization and analysis. Perception is conditioned by external factors, such as climate, drugs, diet, family relationships, and specific environmental configurations. Perception is also influenced by inner-conditioning factors, such as heredity and past experience (Selye, 1975).

Each individual has a different perceptual set on environmental stimuli, which is the reason why each individual reacts differently to the same
stressors. Selye (1975) has pointed out that this is also why several different types of environmental stimuli can induce the same general adaptation syndrome or set of physiological reactions. The key element is
each individual's perception concerning whether or not a stimulus is potentially threatening.

Response patterns. The model presented in Fig. 1 is behavioral. It
directs one to deal with the overt behavior of an individual rather than to
infer a motive or trait. Our intent is to optimize behavior rather than to
analyze motives for behaving.

Psychological energy. A basic assumption, relative to psychological
energy, is that energy can be increased. This is supported by the concept
of "lateral thinking," which assists a person to survive a stressful situation (deBono, 1971). Sometimes the logic system is too constricting in
terms of what appear to be available options, which debilitates creativity
and energy in transcending a problem situation. In other words, "more
may be less." With psychological energy this appears to be true. For example, students have reported that when they feel stressed because of
exams or term paper deadlines, they can derive energy from fellow students through discussion and joint work sessions. Students report that
collective energy increases and they are no longer as exhausted by the
thoughts of approaching deadlines.

Personal experience as a teacher has confirmed the multiplier effect
of given energy. Coming to a large lecture hall filled with eager graduate
students after spending a night up with a teething baby is physically and
mentally draining. It has been my experience, however, that the exhaustion soon leaves after becoming involved in the teaching process and giving energy. Students begin to return the energy until a feeling of replen-
ishment results. This phenomenon has been reported by professionals
when they report for work at 7 AM, make rounds on their patients, and
give nursing care. After making rounds and giving care, it is not uncom-
mon for a nurse to feel recharged. By putting more stress or strain on
one's body in giving to others, sometimes one can reduce feelings of
tiredness and depletion. More can be less.

Stress and professional energy. Selye (1975) has suggested that
there are two perceptual evaluations of stress by individuals: positive
stress called "eustress" and negative stress called "distress." Positive
stress energizes people and helps them continue to heightened awareness and performance capabilities. Negative stress, on the other hand,
depletes energy reserves and taxes the bodily systems in terms of maintenance and defense. Negative, maladaptive responses to stress will

eventually deplete the vital energy store. Selye believes this core of "adaptive energy" is finite in the physiological sense. Depletion will lead eventually to death. Positive stress, on the other hand, energizes and enables a person to move to higher plateaus of performance.

MODEL OF STRESS MANAGEMENT PROCESSES

The model presented in Fig. 1 focuses on four major phases: input, cognitive appraisal, response, and consequence. Feedback to the system can be described in terms of increased or decreased environmental demands.

Case of the noisy ventilator—application of the model

Environmental demands produce stimuli that are perceived as favorable or unfavorable. In the environment of the intensive care unit, there are many environmental demands on the intensive care nurse and other health professionals. For example, a noisy ventilator places demands on the sensory gating capacities[1] of the intensive care nurse and the patients for whom she is caring.[2] The stimulus that affects the intensive care nurse's actions most directly would be restlessness of the patients caused by the unusual noise level of the ventilator. Noting the stimulus of patient restlessness, the nurse appraises whether it is threatening to the well-being of the patients or to her own well-being as a professional in that room. If she perceives the restlessness as nonthreatening, she may do nothing about it. If, on the other hand, she perceives the restlessness as threatening to the patients and to herself, her body is placed on the alert, and she reacts accordingly. Physiologically, she begins to exhibit the general adaptation syndrome of alarm, resistance, and exhaustion (Selye, 1956). Psychologically, she begins to be concerned about pa-

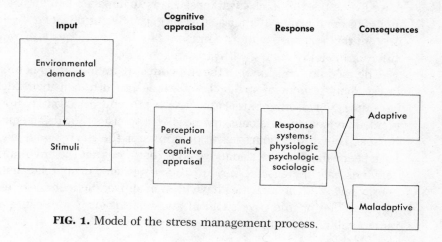

FIG. 1. Model of the stress management process.

tient care and develops intellectual coping mechanisms. Sociologically, she is concerned with the effects of the noise on interpersonal relationships with patients and colleagues, as well as on nursing interventions.

Based on her cognitive appraisal of the situation, the nurse then selects an action. This action is either adaptive or maladaptive. Maladaptive responses deplete her energy reserves and add to the environmental demands made on her. In the case of the noisy ventilator, the nurse may decide to call the engineering personnel. If she is told that an engineer is unavailable and she will have to wait several hours, she may decide to do nothing further. This action may be maladaptive in terms of depleting her own energy stores and those of the patients. If the nurse decides to sedate the patients so that they are no longer overtly restless, the sedation may have negative effects on them.

The nurse may, on the other hand, begin to think about problem solving and how she might alleviate the effects of the constant noise level. For example, if she knows that both of the patients in the room have an interest in music, although they come from widely diverse backgrounds, she might choose to turn on a radio and select a pleasant station to drown out the groaning noise of the ventilator. If this adaptive response is effective, the nurse will find that the restlessness may eventually subside and her own sense of tension will be relieved.

Skill training model

The model presented in Fig. 1 enabled us to develop a training program around the three basic components of an instructional system: presentation, practice, and feedback. In a stress management training program the presentation component involves sensitization to the nature of the environmental demands and the specific stimuli that are usually perceived as stressful. This awareness leads to broader perceptual judgments in appraising whether a stressor is positive or negative. By focusing on the response pattern, nurses can be encouraged to practice different modes of coping with stressful stimuli.

The modules presented in the Appendix are an important component in the management of stress. They are designed to sensitize intensive care nurses and other nurses to certain procedures in stress management. The focus on the consequences of responses provides feedback to nurses. They are encouraged to determine if their actions or reactions have been adaptive or maladaptive and whether or not the environmental demands have increased. They are also encouraged to appraise their own energy levels. If the activities have been adaptive, the feelings of tension will subside and the psychological and physiological well-being of the nurses will have been protected.

The model can assist nurses to evaluate environmental demands and to appraise whether or not these demands are threatening or nonthreatening to a patient or to themselves. Response patterns can be analyzed in terms of the effectiveness of the coping and management strategies.

SUMMARY

This chapter has presented the reader with a conceptual model to describe a stress management process. Our concern was with the management of reactions to stressors in high-tension occupations such as nursing. The specific focus has been stress management for intensive care nurses. Our research, described more fully in Chapter 6, indicated that those areas of greatest emotional pressure and also greatest satisfaction for almost 1800 intensive care nurses concerned interactions with other persons. Our model therefore is psychosocial in nature. Job-related stressors seem to revolve around people problems. *Perceptions* of environmental demands and adaptive or maladaptive responses appear to be key elements in the interactive process between nurses and their environment.

NOTES

1. These are capacities within the human brain that allow a person to filter out "noise" from the content of interest in environmental stimuli. Sensory "gating" allows a person to carry on a conversation on a busy street corner or to concentrate on writing a poem at the seashore.
2. The example of the noisy ventilator was furnished by an intensive care unit nurse, Judith Ann Moran, and represents an actual experience in caring for patients.

REFERENCES

Bailey, J. T., & Claus, K. E. *Decision making in nursing: Tools for change.* St. Louis: C. V. Mosby, 1975.

Claus, K. E., & Bailey, J. T. *Power and influence in health care.* St. Louis: C. V. Mosby, 1977.

deBono, E. *Lateral thinking for management: A handbook for creativity.* New York: American Management Association, 1971.

Festinger, L. *A theory of cognitive dissonance.* Stanford, Calif.: Stanford University Press, 1957.

Heider, F. *The psychology of interpersonal relationships.* New York: Wiley, 1958.

Lazarus, R. S. The concepts of stress and disease. In Levi, L. (Ed.), Society, stress and disease. Vol. I. *The psychosocial environment and psychosomatic disease.* London: Oxford University Press, 1971.

Selye, H. *The stress of life* (2nd ed.). New York: McGraw-Hill, 1976.

Selye, H. *Stress without distress.* New York: Signet Books, 1975.

CHAPTER 3

Job stress and other stress-related problems

June T. Bailey

A rapidly changing society, advanced technology, ever-increasing knowledge, and a profession undergoing both "revolution and evolution" are indeed threatening and stress producing to the nurse. Nevertheless, it seems important to recognize that stress can be a friend or a foe. Eustress ("good stress"), as pointed out in the previous chapter, is a necessary part of human lives to bring about planned change, increased productivity, and personal growth. As Selye (1976) points out, when stress ceases to be a factor in the lives of human beings, they are dead. However, when stress becomes harmful to their well-being and performance (distress), they need to find ways to manage it more effectively.

This chapter will focus primarily on the dimensions of the nurse's job that cause distress. The terms "stress" and "stressor" are used interchangeably to connote distress.

JOB STRESS DEFINED

Job stress has been defined as "the condition in which some factor or combination of factors at work interact with the worker to disrupt his psychological or physiological homeostasis" (Margolis & Kroes, 1974, p. 15). Within this framework the concept of job stress appears to be nebulous, complex, and difficult to access. Another difficulty is that nurses *perceive* stressors in their work environment differently. For example, an event or environmental demand on the nurse, such as responding to a "Code Blue," may present a challenge to one nurse, whereas another nurse may perceive it as extremely stressful, which will be discussed in Part Two. The nurse's perception of the event or demand and the intensity of the demand, as described by Selye (1979), are key elements in job-related stress in nursing. However, one also needs to recognize that individual differences, such as hereditary factors, early childhood experiences, cultural patterns, and health status, are among an infinite number of variables which determine the stress level of nurses and how they respond to it.

JOB STRESS AS "BURNOUT"

Job stress is frequently referred to in the literature as "burnout" on the job (Freudenberger, 1974; Maslach, 1979; Pines & Maslach, 1978; Shubin, 1978). Burnout is characterized by physical, emotional, and spiritual exhaustion. Within the framework of stress, burnout has been described as a process that "involves the loss of concern with whom one is working" (Maslach, 1979, p. 113). To a large measure it contributes to the inadequate delivery of health care.

A common response to burnout is for the person to resign and possibly leave the profession. To cope with burnout, Maslach (1979) suggests that support systems for health professionals be established, humor be used more judiciously and extensively, interpersonal skills be established, and health maintenance be improved.

Characteristics of burnout

Burnout is characterized by a greatly reduced energy level. The individual may suffer from feelings of alienation as evidenced by withdrawing from work and other groups and interests. There is a tendency to exhibit negative feelings toward others, characterized by cynical and derogatory remarks. The individual may also begin to suspect and blame others. Burnout appears to be a factor in lowered morale, absenteeism, and lowered work performance as well as physical signs and symptoms of illness.

Nurses as potential candidates for burnout

Anderson (1979) points out that prime candidates for job burnout are new employees whose high expectations and educational preparation are not being met in the work world. This is also borne out by Kramer's work (1974). Other prime candidates for the burnout syndrome are those whose job involves close interaction with others. Nurses certainly fit into both these categories, as will be clear when the nature of the nurse's job is reviewed.

NATURE OF NURSING PRACTICE

Although a number of definitions of nursing practice exist, a widely accepted one is that of an eminent nurse theoretician, who conceptualized the function of the nurse as follows: "The nature of nursing is to assist the individual, sick or well, in the performance of those activities contributing to health or its recovery (or to peaceful death) that he would perform unaided if he had the necessary strength, will or knowledge" (Henderson, 1964, p. 8). Those of us in nursing realize that the nature of our work requires us to become deeply involved in the field of human behavior. Sympathy, understanding, compassion, competence, judgment, and *personal* involvement in the lives and deaths of other human beings are key elements in the caring, professional nursing role. These intense interactions with the patient, as well as personal involvement and interactions with the patients' families or "significant others," members of the health care team, administrators, and the community, can indeed be precursors to stresses and strains for nurses, irrespective of their position or setting.

WORK SETTING

In addition to the nature of nursing as a potential stressor, the majority of nurses work in hospitals, which for the most part are emotionally charged environments. Noxious agents such as bacteria and viruses, threats of nuclear radiation, crowded work spaces, and unpleasant odors represent some of the environmental factors with which nurses must contend and which are addressed in Chapter 9.

NURSE-ENVIRONMENT FIT

One of the primary factors in job stress is poor "person-environment fit" (French & Caplan, 1973). According to these investigators, one factor of person-environment fit related to job stress includes the degree to which a person's abilities and skills match the requirements on the job and the job demands. Another factor is the extent to which workers are encouraged and permitted to use their knowledge and skills in the job settings. French (1974) maintains that either or both of the factors just described can cause job stress. Depression, psychosomatic illness, and job dissatisfaction are primary effects of job stress on the worker.

Role conflict and role ambiguity are concepts similar to French and Caplan's (1973) concepts of job-environment fit. The untoward effect of the role conflict on nurses is well studied and documented in the nursing literature (Benner & Kramer, 1972; Kramer, 1974; La Rocco, 1978).

McLean (1974) has also pointed out that where excessive and conflicting information about one's expected role is present, role conflict and ultimately stress among the worker are likely to occur. This is particularly relevant in nursing. For example, new and expanded roles in nursing with nebulous job descriptions, unclear staff-line relationships, and inadequate measures of job performance reflect situations in the nurse's work world that lead to stress and dissatisfaction.

MANIFESTATIONS OF JOB STRESS

Stresses and strains incurred by nurses in the performance of their nursing role can be manifested in a number of ways. The following indicators may be helpful in looking at potential signs and symptoms of stressors (Margolis & Kroes, 1974; Pelletier, 1977; Pines & Maslach, 1978).

Behavioral indicators

- Decreased productivity and quality-of-job performance
- Tendency to make mistakes—poor judgment
- Forgetfulness and blocking
- Diminished attention to detail
- Preoccupation—daydreaming or "spacing out"
- Inability to concentrate on tasks
- Reduced creativity
- Increased use of alcohol and/or drugs
- Increased smoking
- Increased absenteeism and illness
- Lethargy
- Loss of interest
- Accident proneness

Physical indicators

- Elevated blood pressure
- Increased muscle tension (neck, shoulders, back)
- Elevated pulse and/or increased respiration
- "Sweaty" palms
- Cold hands and feet
- Slumped posture
- Tension headache
- Upset stomach
- Higher pitched voice
- Change in appetite
- Urinary frequency
- Restlessness—difficulty in falling asleep or frequent awakening

Emotional indicators

- Emotional outbursts and crying
- Irritability
- Depression
- Withdrawal
- Hostile and assaultive behavior
- Tendency to blame others

- Anxiousness
- Feeling of worthlessness
- Suspiciousness

It should be pointed out that the indicators that have been presented are gross measures and need to be looked at from behavioral, physical, and emotional dimensions. Since individuals manifest the effects of work overload in different ways (Levinson, 1970), the categories of symptoms and the various indicators presented should be reviewed with this in mind.

OTHER STRESS-RELATED JOB PROBLEMS

It is difficult to separate one's professional role from the dimensions of one's personal life. As a consequence, it is important to recognize that the stress indicators which have been presented may not be entirely due to job-related stress.

Life events

Stressful life events may be precursors to stress-related symptoms and to physical or psychological illness. Holmes and Rahe (1967) developed a Social Readjustment Rating Scale (SRRS), which rates the potential impact of life events on the individual. At the top of the list is the death of a spouse. The authors contend that the more changes which occur at one time in the life of the individual, and the nature of the changes, the more likely the individual is to become vulnerable to illness.

Personality patterns

In addition to the changes going on in one's personal and professional life, the personality patterns of the individual need to be considered (Howard, Cunningham, & Rechnitzer, 1976). As Dunn (1977, p. 10) points out, "The individual is a total personality consisting of a continuum of body, mind, and spirit within an ever-changing environment and flow of events." The way in which the event is interpreted by the individual and the resultant behavior or response are key concepts in determining the level of stress (Selye, 1974).

Friedman and Rosenman (1974) have identified a behavior pattern known as the "coronary-prone behavior pattern," which they contend is associated with elevated blood pressure and also highly related to coronary heart disease. The syndrome is also known as "type A behavior." The authors state that the behavior pattern is not related entirely to the individual's personality but that rapid changes, challenges, and conditions of contemporary society also impact on this behavioral syndrome.

Briefly, an individual who exhibits type A behavior has a high need for achievement, is constantly competitive, dominates conversations, is in chronic conflict with people, is impatient, tends to interrupt others, sets a fast work pace with a sense of time pressure, and appears to be unable to relax and enjoy the "fruits of his labor."

In contrast, that person with "type B behavior" is easygoing, has little sense of time urgency, experiences few conflicts with others, and usually sociable and likable. Friedman and Roseman (1974) have indicated in their study of some 3500 men that individuals who exhibit type A behavior are from one to five times more susceptible to coronary heart disease.

UNTOWARD EFFECTS OF JOB STRESS

It is beyond the scope of this chapter to deal extensively with job stress and precisely how it correlates with work performance. Work performance largely depends on those who are defining and evaluating the job performance of the worker. Performance criteria and the assessment tools that are used constitute other important dimensions. We recognize that evaluation of quality patient care services is one of the weakest links in the delivery of care. However, there is evidence that job stress does lower performance (Pines & Maslach, 1978) and that it frequently accounts for the high attrition rate of nurses (Nader, 1972; Razem, 1974). Job stress and its relationship to work performance and to the health status of the worker have become a matter of national concern. Causal relationships between stress and illness are well documented (Garfield, 1979; Pelletier, 1977; Selye, 1976) and will be presented in Part Three.

SUMMARY

This chapter has presented the concept of job-related stress from a number of perspectives and frames of reference. The purpose is twofold: (1) to serve as a backdrop for the chapters that follow, in an effort to alert the reader to the complexity and difficulties in dealing with job stress, and (2) to present an overview of the elements of the nurse's work world, and in their personal lives, that make them particularly vulnerable to stress.

The indicators and effects of job stress and other stress-related problems are conceptualized as dependent on a wide range of intervening variables. Among the more important are the intensity, frequency, and general nature of the stressor; the *perceptions* of the nurse relative to the stressor; life events; personality and cultural patterns; health status; and the responses of the individual to the stressors.

REFERENCES

Anderson, E. Too much "stewing" leads to job "burn-out." *The Peninsula Times Tribune.* Wednesday, June 20, 1979, p. D-6.

Benner, P., & Kramer, M. Role conceptions and integrative role behavior of nurses in special care and regular hospital nursing units. *Nursing Research,* 1972, *21,* 20-29.

Dunn, H. What high level wellness means. *Health Values: Achieving High Level Wellness,* 1977, *1*(1), 9-16.

French, J. Person role fit. In A. McLean (Ed.), *Occupational stress.* Springfield, Ill.: Charles C Thomas, 1974.

French, J., & Caplan, R. Organizational stress and individual strain. In A. Morrow (Ed.), *The failure of success.* New York: AMACOM, 1973.

Freudenberger, H. Staff burn-out. *Journal of Social Issues,* 1974, *30,* 159-165.

Friedman, M., & Rosenman, R. *Type A behavior and your heart.* New York: Alfred A. Knopf, 1974.

Garfield, C. *Stress and survival.* St. Louis: C. V. Mosby, 1979.

Henderson, V. The nature of nursing. In M. Meyers (Ed.), *Nursing fundamentals.* Dubuque, Iowa: W. C. Brown, 1964.

Holmes, T., & Rahe, R. The Social Readjustment Rating Scale. *Journal of Psychosomatic Research,* 1967, *11,* 213-218.

Howard, J., Cunningham, D., & Rechnitzer, P. Health patterns associated with Type A behavior: A managerial population. *Journal of Human Stress,* 1976, *2*(1), 24-31.

Kramer, M. *Reality shock.* St. Louis: C. V. Mosby, 1974.

La Rocco, S. An introduction to role theory for nurses. *Supervisor Nurse,* 1978, *9*(12), 41-45.

Levinson, H. *Executive stress.* New York: Harper & Row, 1970.

Margolis, B., & Kroes, W. Occupational stress and strain. In A. McLean, (Ed.), *Occupational stress.* Springfield, Ill.: Charles C Thomas, 1974.

Maslach, C. The burn-out syndrome in patient care. In C. Garfield, (Ed.), *Stress and survival.* St. Louis: C. V. Mosby, 1979.

McLean, A. *Occupational stress.* Springfield, Ill.: Charles C Thomas, 1974.

Nader, A. (Ed.). ICU '72: A survey of the intensive care units and coronary care units in 1,111 short-term general hospitals with 100 or more beds. *RN Magazine,* Research department, Oradell, N.J., 1972.

Pelletier, K. *Mind as healer: Mind as slayer.* New York: Delacorte, 1977.

Pines, A., & Maslach, C. Characteristics of staff burn-out in mental health settings. *Hospital and Community Psychiatry,* 1978, *29,* 233-237.

Razem, J. Nursing turnover in special care units. *Abstracts of Hospital Management Studies,* 1974, *10,* 335.

Selye, H. *Stress without distress.* New York: Signet Books, 1974.

Selye, H. *Stress in health and disease.* Woburn, Mass. Butterworths, 1976.

Seyle, H. *The stress of my life* (2nd ed.). New York: Van Nostrand-Reinhold, 1979.

Shubin, S. Burn-out: The professional hazard you face in nursing. *Nursing 78,* 1978, *8*(7), 22-27.

SUGGESTED READINGS

Holland, J., Sgroi, S., Marwit, S., & Solkoff, N. The ICU syndrome: Fact or fancy. *International Journal of Psychiatry in Medicine,* 1973, *4,* 241-249.

Kahn, R., et al. *Organizational stress: Studies in role conflict and ambiguity.* New York: Wiley, 1964.

Lazarus, R. *Psychological stress and the coping process.* New York: McGraw-Hill, 1966.

Levi, L. (Ed.). *Society, stress and disease — The psychosocial environment and psychosomatic diseases.* London: Oxford University Press, 1971.

McLean, A. *Mental health and work organization.* Chicago: Rand McNally, 1970.

Mechanic, D. *Future issues in health care.* New York: Free Press, 1979.

Menzies, I. E. P. Nurses under stress. *International Nursing Review,* 1960, *7*(6), 9-16.

Rabkin, J., & Struening, E. Life events, stress and illness. *Science,* 1976, *194,* 1013-1020.

Selye, H. *The stress of life* (2nd ed.). New York: McGraw-Hill, 1976.

PART TWO

Stressors in the intensive care unit

CHAPTER 4

No time for tenderness: a day in the life of an ICU nurse

Jan MacLachlan

The alarm rings, and I roll over to look at the clock. It is 5:15 in the morning. Strange, it seems like I just fell asleep, and now it's time to get ready for work again. I wish I didn't have to work today; I am tired, and it's still dark outside. The temptation to call in sick passes, though, and I begin to dress and make some coffee. By 6:15 I am ready to go. Driving to work, I think about what my assignment might be for the day. I wonder if I'll care for one of the heart transplant patients? Maybe I'll be assigned to one of the long-term patients, or perhaps I'll receive a postoperative patient from the OR. Then again, I may be a float nurse today.[1] It is now 6:35, and I begin to look for a parking place in the already overfilled lot.

While waiting in the coffee room for report and the rest of the staff to arrive, I have another cup of coffee. Thank God for coffee! When the charge nurses arrive, assignments are given out and a brief report occurs. I have been assigned two patients today, a woman (Mrs. L) just extubated on two intravenous drips who needs pulmonary care, and a man (Mr. T) ready for transfer. I wonder if I will get the first surgical case of the day? Report is over, and I go off to my room with my Kardexes. The night nurse is just finishing helping Mrs. L, who has had a triple vessel CABG (coronary-artery bypass graft) and is still rather drowsy, but alert and oriented. She is doing well, though her lungs are still fairly congested, and her blood pressure is a bit labile. She is on dopamine for perfusion and lidocaine for PVCs (premature ventricular contractions). She has been bathed and bed changed, but there is blood all over where the doctors pulled her chest tubes. Typical!

I copy my Kardexes and go over Mr. L's postextubation orders, and then I get ready to start the day. My float nurse comes in to see if I need anything. There is nothing yet. It's time for Mrs. L's 7:30 signs. The patient is in SR (sinus rhythm), a few PVCs. She is neurologically intact, breath sounds diminished in the bases, and a few rales scattered throughout. Her dressings need changing, abdomen is soft, faint bowel sounds are present, Foley catheter is in, urine is dropping off. Blood pressure is good; I wonder if I can wean the dopamine and lidocaine down (both are at minimum rates)? There are no orders. The doctors are already in OR; I will have to catch them between cases. Mr T's signs are stable. His lungs are clear but decreased in right base; he needs to be tactfully encouraged to turn, cough, and deep breathe. The night nurse spent a lot of time working with him. He has been bathed, weighed, and all of his dressings changed. Also, the IV bottle and tubing are new— what a tremendous help all of that is to me. I silently thank her for her excellent nursing care. Mrs. L needs postextubation gases done, and I call out to the desk and am told that the blood gas technician was just there and won't be back for another half hour. I wonder if there is a bed on E2A (in the intermediate care unit) for Mr. T? He is wondering, too, but we won't know until float report.[2]

It's 8 o'clock now and time for Mrs. L's signs again. The EKG technician arrives. The clerk calls in the 5 AM lab results; Mrs. L's K^+ (potassium) is only 3.4 mEq. Maybe her PVCs are related to the low K, and she needs to be replaced to 5 mEq instead of the routinely ordered 4.5 mEq? I will have to remember to ask the doctors about that when I see them. Mr. T needs to go to the bathroom, and I walk him there. He is steady on his feet, though his leg incision is oozing. I'll have to change the dressings later. Mrs. L is complaining of incisional pain, and I call out to the desk for morphine. Mr. T is through in the bathroom and wants to go back to bed. I explain the need for him to sit in the chair for his respiratory treatment. His breakfast will be coming soon, too. He agrees to sit in the chair, and the IT (inhalation therapist) arrives to give him his breathing treatment. Back to Mrs. L. The morphine still isn't here, and I call out to the desk again. Her dopamine is running out, as well. The blood gas technician arrives to do her ABGs (arterial blood gases). I draw the blood gases and get the new dopamine mixed. Here is my float, who asks if I want a break. Do I! On my way out, I tell my charge nurse that I think Mrs. L may need a higher K^+ replacement and that we need orders to wean her drips off. She will pass it on to the doctors if she sees them or will send them in. I also get the MS (morphine sulfate).

In the coffee room for a break, I have another cup of coffee. There is some small talk and, as usual, a few stories being told. I am beginning to feel awake now. Back to my room; my float has shaved Mr. T and done Mrs. L's 8:30 signs and also has drawn my 9 o'clock blood work. There is nothing like a good float! Now it's time to help Mrs. L with her bath and hygiene care. I'll have to change her IV bottles and tubing as well. With all this completed, I get her into the chair. She is wobbly on her feet, but the two of us manage. Breakfast arrives. Mrs. L is not hungry and wants to go back to bed. I encourage her to stay sitting in the chair for 15 more minutes. It's 9 AM and the respiratory therapist arrives for Mrs. L's IPPB treatment. I wonder if I'm going to get a first case as I change the bed linens. I need assistance helping Mrs. L return to bed because she feels weak. She wants to lie on her right side, and just after I've gotten her settled, the CXR (chest x-ray) technician arrives. I should know by now not to position a patient till the CXR is done. Mr. T is ready to go back to bed, too, and I help him.

It's 9:30, and I learn that I *am* getting a first case. Mr. S is a man in his forties with coronary artery disease and aortic stenosis. He could be unstable. Mr. T has a bed on E2A at 10:30 AM. It's time to begin to set up the necessary equipment for the postoperative heart patient. Also, I have to get Mr. T's belongings together. Mrs. L is stable, and I suspect I can do her signs hourly. Her urine is low, though, and so is her CVP (central venous pressure), which is 7; we have orders to keep it at 10 to 15. Maybe she needs a little SPA (salt-poor albumen) and saline. Her PCV (packed cell volume) is 37, so she doesn't need blood; the charge nurse agrees. The unit clerk brings me the SPA. My float comes in and gets Mr. T ready for transfer, so I can start setting up for my case. The clerk calls in to say that I can call report on Mr. T. But the nurse on E2A is on break, and I will have to call back later. I feel my frustration beginning to rise. Visiting hours are in 15 minutes. I take 10 o'clock signs for Mrs. L. She is stable, but her urine output remains low; it's only 20 ml per hour. The clerk calls back to say that we have a 45-minute call on my case. Great— I now have two patients in the room, still have to transfer Mr. T, and have not begun to set up for the new patient. I call E2A; the nurse is there, and I give her my report and say we will be bringing the patient over soon. At least Mrs. L is sleeping. Visitors begin to arrive. Mr. T's family is here. I explain that he is doing well and no longer needs intensive care. We are transferring him to another room. My float assists him into a wheelchair and transports him to his new unit. I call out to the desk for housekeeping to clean his space so I can move Mrs. L to Mr. T's space. (The new patient always gets the bed closest to the supplies.)

The clerk calls in my 9 AM lab results. Mrs. L's K$^+$ is still running low, but at least her urine output is picking up. Her family is here. I explain to them that she is doing well and will be moved to another bed, since we are getting a patient from the OR. I wish I had more time to talk to them and offer some reassurance. Finally, I start my setup: blood warmer, blood pump, blood tape,[3] arterial line transducer, alcohol swabs, maintenance

IV bottle, thermometer, teleprobe. The OR porter arrives with my anesthesia report sheet, and I discover that the patient has a Swan-Ganz catheter, which means that two more transducer setups must be prepared. He is also on dopamine, Nipride, and lidocaine and should be arriving from OR in 20 minutes. My float is back and between the two of us, we move Mrs. L. over to the other bed space and get ready for Mr. S. Has anything been forgotten? Yes, we still need tubing to connect the chest tubes to suction, as well as two suction bottles. Housekeeping is cleaning the bed space, and IT is setting up the respirator.

My float releases me for a break. On my way to the coffee room, I ask the clerks to let me know when we have a 5-minute call from the OR. There is time for a quick cup of coffee and a cigarette, then the call comes and I go back to the room. The unit clerks call in Mr. S's ABGs from the OR. They are not very good. His coags (blood coagulation studies) are off, too, and I wonder whether he is bleeding. The clerk calls; Mr. S is on his way. The patient is accompanied by the resident, anesthesia, and the OR porters. Here we go! IT is ready to hook up Mr. S to the respirator. I attach him up to the monitor; he is in SR and my float hooks up the chest tubes and takes his temperature. His MAP (mean arterial pressure) is in the 60s, and the doctors are asking for the CVP and PAD (pulmonary artery diastolic pressure) readings. The IV bottles and tubing are tangled in a big knot, and I have a suspicion that anesthesia macrames the tubing on the way from the OR. The charge nurse arrives and gives us a hand. We listen to the anesthesiologist while he gives his report, as we untangle the tubes and figure out which is which, get the blood hooked up to the warmer, the NG (nasogastric) tube positioned, bottles hung, drips counted, CVP taken, temperature taken, chest tubes stripped, PAD done, and arterial line hooked to transducers. This is not easy with two anesthesiologists hovering over the patient and IT hooking up the ventilator.

Meanwhile, the clerk is calling lab results over the intercom and asking if we are ready for the CXR and ABGs. Who are they kidding? Finally, things begin to look a bit more organized, and I wish that everyone would clear out so I could get my orders copied and my patient assessed. It is now 11 AM. The doctors leave, and my float does the patient's vital signs. They are to be taken every 20 minutes for the first 12 hours. While she does that, I copy the orders and skim the chart. Mr. S has had a double vessel CABG and an AVR (aortic valve replacement). He has been relatively stable in the OR, though there has been some problem with bleeding. His coags are off, and he's receiving some FFP (fresh frozen plasma). Because the patient has had a history of VT (ventricular tachycardia) and has been on Pronestyl at home, the lidocaine drip is prophylactic. The doctors have not ordered Pronestyl, however, and I remember to mention it to them or the ACNC (assistant clinical nursing coordinator). His K^+ is to be replaced to 5. CVP is to be kept at 12 to 18, MAP at 70 to 85, and no minimum drip orders. My float leaves for lunch. It has been a busy day for her, as well. I start my 11:20 signs. X-ray rolls in to do the CXR, and the blood gas technician arrives. I might as well send a K^+ and PCV too. His K^+ from the OR was 5; his last PCV was 32, but he has had a unit of blood since then.

At last, everyone has left. I finish vital signs and start my assessment. Mr. S is still well anesthetized. His color is good, the skin cold and dry, temperature 35°—all routine. Patients are always cold coming out of surgery. He will warm gradually. My float drops off some warm blankets. Pedal pulses are present. NG is patent, and there is good air entry bilaterally to the lungs, which are clear. Chest tubes are draining moderate amounts of sanguineous fluid. He has drained 100 cc of blood since his return from OR. I finish the FFP, then send for some more coags. Mrs. L is awake now. I check her vital signs and drip rates. She has had no PVCs all morning. Her blood pressure is good, and urine output is much improved since the fluid bolus. Her dopamine is at a minimum rate now. The resident comes in and I ask him for orders. He disappears again. I can wean the dopamine and lidocaine off and replace her K^+ to 5.

It is 11:40, time for vital signs again. Mr. S is starting to warm, and his MAP also is going up as he begins to shiver. His temperature has gone from 35° to 36° in 20 minutes, and his MAP is now 110. Because a MAP reading this high could possibly cause a graft to rupture, I gradually turn up the Nipride. I consider turning the dopamine off but decide to leave it at a minimum rate, since his MAP will become labile as he warms. He is still bleeding from his CTs (chest tubes); his platelets come back at 50 (50,000) k.[4] The clinical nurse coordinator (CNC) is aware and paging the doctors for orders. He continues to shiver so I give 5 mg MS IV and 5 mg Valium IV, which helps some.

Now the pink lady, as we call the auxiliary women, comes to see if the family can visit. Somehow I'd rather they didn't because Mr. S is somewhat labile, but I realize how very anxious they must be. The family comes in nervously, accompanied by the pink lady, and I introduce myself, explaining that I will be with the patient until I leave at 3 PM, when another nurse will take over. Mrs. S is somewhat teary. I silently hope that she will not faint. Her son is with her, and they cautiously approach the bed. Mr. S is stable, and I encourage them to touch and talk to him. They ask the usual questions: "Can he hear us?" "When will he wake up?" "Why is he shaking?" "Why is he so puffy?" I explain that he may be able to hear and that persons wake up at their own rate, depending on the anesthesia and their tolerance to it. I also reassure them that he is in no pain and will be kept well sedated for the first few hours. He is shaking because he is warming up; everyone does it. The puffiness is due to fluid replacements and shifts during surgery; it may even increase but will gradually diminish in the next couple of days. I notice his MAP is now in the low 60s and try, nonchalantly, to turn his Nipride down and pump some blood in, noting that his temperature is now 36.5°, which means that he is starting to vasodilate. I review the various lines and tubings with the family. They remember some from the preoperative teaching class. It is 12 o'clock now—time for vital signs. I request that the family leave for a while so I can complete my work. I assure them that everything is going well and that they can come back to see him in an hour.

The unit clerk brings in the 1 PM blood slips, and the ACNC calls in to say that the doctor has ordered 6 units of platelets and repeat coags after. Mrs. S wants to know what they are for. I explain that being on bypass can sometimes alter the normal clotting mechanisms in the blood. Mr. S's are slightly off, and we are merely correcting them. After the family leaves, I suction Mr. S. His ABGs come back and are very good. The ACNC and I discuss changes on the respirator setting; IT comes in and makes the changes.

Meanwhile, Mr. S's MAP is fluctuating. His CVP is down to 8, and his chest tubes are still draining about 100 cc per hour. I pump in more blood. His PCV comes back 34. He seems to be draining his blood volume out as fast as it is given. He is now having some PCVs—too frequently, I think. I ask the clerks what the patient's K^+ is, and they promise to check. Until the results come back, I decide to put 10 mEq of potassium chloride in the Volutrol. Also, I call for blood gases. The blood is running out, and the platelets have not arrived. I call the desk again. The clerks will check. Meanwhile, I order another unit of blood.

I can feel myself getting frustrated again and irritable. I need a break. Where is my float? Time for 12:20 vital signs: MAP, 65; CVP, 9; still some PVCs, dopamine at 16 gtt per minute, Nipride at 10 gtt, and still pushing volume. The patient's temperature is now 37.5°. IT arrives for Mrs.'s respiratory treatment. I feel as though I've not been spending much time with her and tell her just to ask if she wants something. We get her up in the chair and start her treatment. Lunch will be arriving soon, too. At 12:30 my float arrives to ask if I am ready for lunch. Am I! I give her a quick rundown of things and then leave, taking my flow sheets with me to chart. It seems as though I've just sat down to eat and it's 1 PM—time to go back.

Mr. S has finally gotten his platelets. His K$^+$ was 3.5; no wonder he was having PVCs. At least his chest tube output is slowing down now. The doctors were in, and we have an order for Pronestyl now, too. ABGs will be coming soon and so will the visitors at 1:15 PM. Time for Keflin. Only 2 more hours to go. Mrs. L is still eating lunch, and I quickly change her bed. The unit clerk calls in to see if my 1 PM blood work is ready yet. It isn't. Mr. S's family arrives and asks whether he is awake. I explain that he is stable and will be asleep for a while yet.

It's now 1:20 PM and time for vital signs again. I am getting tired of stripping chest tubes. Mrs. L's visitors tell me that she wants to go back to bed. I finish taking signs and am getting Mrs. L back in bed when the blood gas technician arrives. Get the gases; get Mrs. L's blood work, and then a quick chat with Mrs. L's family—she is doing very well; her drips are off, and her heart rate is regular; yes, she may get transferred tomorrow if there's a bed. It's time to suction Mr. S again. His family leaves. As I advance the suction catheter into his ET (endotracheal) tube, Mr. S starts to awaken. I tell him to relax and that his operation is over; he is in the ICU, and everything is fine. He nods, and I give him another 3 mg morphine and 5 mg Valium IV. Gradually, Mr. S drifts off to sleep again. I send off his K$^+$, then another PCV and coags. My new unit of blood is here, and I need someone to check it with me. I look up and down the hall; it is empty. There never seems to be anyone around when you need them.

I call out to the desk for my float and take the 1:40 vital signs. Chest drainage is slowing; CVP, 10; MAP, 70; turn the Nipride down a bit. Temperature is 38.5°. My float arrives. We check the blood and hook up the unit. I want to change the bed; it's a mess. I explain to Mr. S what we are going to do. In the middle of changing the bed, the clerks call in the lab results. I will have to call them back.

It is 2 PM. Mr. S looks comfortable. After 1000 cc of blood and 6 units of platelets, he seems more stable. ABGs are adequate; we won't change his respirator settings. His drips are now at a fixed rate. I get 2 PM vital signs on him while my float gets Mrs. L's. Time for a break and then a report for the charge nurse before I leave. Another quick coffee and a smoke. I finish my notes and go back to the room. My float has tidied up and has my intake and output done. Great! Half an hour to go. Both patients look good, and the room is neat. Despite all my frustration and worry, I feel a sense of satisfaction. The evening shift begins to arrive. I hope there is no in-service today; I want to leave on time. Time for 2:40 signs. I have gotten very tired of doing vital signs every 20 minutes but finish them, pump more blood, strip the chest tubes, and finish charting.

It's now 3 PM. I finish the report, say goodbye to my patients, and wish the nurse a good evening. Walking out the door, I am tired but satisfied with the last 8 hours. I think about what I am going to do when I get home, and decide to go to the spa to relax. A workout, sauna, and swim, and home again—pleasantly tired and relaxed. Supper, then it's time to get things ready for work tomorrow. Only one more day before the weekend. Maybe I should call in sick. But on second thoughts, I set the alarm for 5:15—the end of a day and almost the beginning of a new day.

NOTES

1. "Float" refers to being assigned to assist other nurses with their patient assignment (i.e., getting necessary equipment, assisting with turning and weighing patients, relieving the nurse when she takes a break or goes to lunch, etc.).
2. The float report is an early morning report in which the charge nurse informs the float nurses which patients will be transferred and into which rooms the new postoperative patients will be admitted.
3. This is an informal, but useful, method of recording the amount of blood replacement that a postoperative patient has received. (It consists of a piece of adhesive tape with gradations of 100 cc marked on it. The tape is suspended from the IV pole, on which the blood bag is hanging. As the patient receives another 100 cc of blood, the tape marker is turned up. Therefore an accurate count of the amount of blood replacement is readily available at all times.)
4. Normal platelet count is 200 to 400 k (200,000 to 400,000/cu mm).

CHAPTER 5

Stress and the ICU nurse: a review of nursing studies

James W. Grout

With the advent of the intensive care unit (ICU) in the early 1960s, attention in the literature was soon directed toward the particular stressors found there. Although several authors (Holsclaw, 1965; Jones, 1962; Menzies, 1960) had spoken of the vulnerability of nurses to stressful situations, Koumans (1965) was one of the first to emphasize the stressors of the ICU. Since then, the psychological stress of the intensive care nurse has been the topic of numerous articles (Bilodeau, 1973; Cassem & Hackett, 1975; Hay & Oken, 1972; Huckabay & Jagla, 1979; Jacobson, 1978; Kornfeld, 1971; Michaels, 1971; Simon & Whiteley, 1977; Strauss, 1968; Vreeland & Ellis, 1969). Often, however, these discussions have centered around a concept of stress that is defined either insufficiently or not at all.

A PROBLEM OF DEFINITION

In the nursing literature, stress usually is regarded as a stimulus and characterized as deriving from a variety of sources: work itself or its environment and equipment, patients and their families, physicians and administrators, or other nurses (e.g., Bilodeau, 1973; Huckabay & Jagla, 1979; Jacobson, 1978; Michaels, 1971). The weakness of such an emphasis is that it requires the researcher to designate a situation as "stress," which, although it may evoke a response in one person, may elicit little or none in another. Indeed, one of the paradoxes of intensive care nursing is that much which is stressful in the unit may also be a source of satisfaction and challenge.

Menzies (1960), for example, considered stress to be a stimulus and regarded it as "a problem of the profession arising from the professional situation rather than a matter of the individual nurse's personality" (p. 9). This same perspective is seen in Gentry, Foster, and Froehling (1972), who found that nurses in two coronary care units had signifi-

33

cantly different levels of affect and likes or dislikes about work, even though the units themselves had similar duties, patients, and physical settings. It was suggested that situational stress might account for the difference, and a lack of adequate help, necessary continuing education, and staff pride were all cited as possible reasons for such disparity. Their conclusion was that "psychologic and emotional stress is a product of the professional situation in which the nurse operates and not her own personality" (p. 796).

Such a definition of stress is limited, however, as can be seen in an article by Cleland (1965), which studied the effect of situational stressors on the performance of nurses. She found that the performance of nurses who indicated a high need for social approval declined with an increase in stressors, whereas that of nurses with a low need increased. In other words, the nurses responded differently to similar situations, not because the situations were different but because *they* were. A definition of stress, then, as stimulus alone is not sufficient, and Cleland's question of "whether the 'stressor' was of real personal significance to each subject, or, was chosen only as being relevant to the experimenter's theoretical position" (p. 292) is an important reminder of that fact.

In the literature, too, stress sometimes is not differentiated from that which causes it, and the same word is used to mean both stimulus *and* response. That problem, which is one of semantics, is avoided by Selye (1950, 1976), who defined stress as "the nonspecific response of the body to any demand" (1976, p. 15). Within that definition was a crucial distinction: the nonspecificity of the body's response, which Selye defined as "stress," and those demands on the body that cause it, which he defined as "stressors." Although every demand made on the body is specific, the body's response to those stressors is nonspecific, for example, the excretion of stress hormones. The mechanism by which this response is mediated was uncertain, however.

Mason (1971, 1975a, 1975b) suggested that this "first mediator" of Selye's stress concept "may simply be the psychological apparatus involved in emotional or arousal reactions" (1971, p. 329). Stress, in other words, should be regarded not so much a physiological concept as a behavioral one. Instead of different stressors, or stimuli, eliciting a common nonspecific hormonal response, Mason proposed that they evoked a nonspecific behavioral response, that of emotional arousal. The significance of Mason's disagreement is that it requires the individual somehow to *perceive* the situation to be stressful for there to be a hormonal response to it.

This perception, or what Lazarus (1977, p. 145) calls "cognitive appraisal," is important to an understanding of stress because responses to a given situational stimulus (or stressor) can vary from individual to individual, or within the same individual from time to time. Such appraisal can determine not only the nature and intensity of an emotional response, but it also underlies the coping mechanisms which continually determine that response to the environment and how it is evaluated. Whether the nurse copes and adapts to the intensive care situation or is overwhelmed by it largely depends on the perceptions of the individual and the interplay of personality and environment rather than on the "professional situation" alone. The competency of the nurse and how one's interaction with the environment is arranged and interpreted are variables that may determine whether there even *is* a stress response.

Stress should not be regarded either as external to the individual and residing only in the social or physical environment or as existing solely within the person as some psychological vulnerability. Nor should the term remain completely undifferentiated so that there is no distinction between stress and the situational factors which cause it. Rather, the stress response is an intimate part of the transaction between personality and environment and is determined largely by the perceptions of the individual. It is the nurse who regards a stressor as threatening or challenging and responds to it. Whether or not the nurse derives satisfaction from working in the ICU is less a matter of being confronted by the stressors of the unit than of how the nurse copes with those factors. This emphasis on the response of the nurse and the ability to change is important, especially since many stressors in the unit may not themselves be susceptible to change.

IMPLICATIONS FOR FUTURE RESEARCH

In some of the suggestions for reducing stress which are found in the literature, it is tacitly admitted that much of what stresses the nurse in the ICU cannot be changed. Often, it is advised, the nurse should simply escape from them by the transfer or periodic rotation to another, nonintensive environment; occasional leave or brief vacations to allow for recuperation; some area away from the unit in which to relax and be temporarily removed from it; or, at least, a regular work schedule to allow for uninterrupted meals and breaks (Bilodeau, 1973; Gardam, 1969; Hay & Oken, 1972; Kornfeld, 1971). Although these recommendations are legitimate and can offer relief from the work situation, they do not change its reality and may only serve to exaggerate the contrast when the nurse returns to the unit.

The solutions that are offered in the literature may not always be possible. Physicians, for example, often are cited as a source of stress for the ICU nurse. Their absence from the unit may cause uncertainty about responsibility and priorities in emergencies, and it is argued that they should be constantly and immediately available to offer treatment and advice in such situations (Bilodeau, 1973; Hay & Oken, 1972; Kornfeld, 1971; Vreeland & Ellis, 1969). One can only remember Menzies' words that if there were a simple solution, it would have been introduced long ago (1960, p. 16).

It may be better to confront the problem of nursing stress in the ICU by reframing it. Watzlawick, Weakland, and Fisch (1974, p. 95) define reframing as a change in the meaning attributed to a situation. Although the situation itself may remain unchanged, there may still be change, if only in the appraisal of it. What is changed by reframing is not the situation but its significance.

Death and dying, for example, are realities of the ICU that cannot be changed. The nurse's perception of them and the attendant feelings of anger, resentment, and guilt may be, however. The response of the nurse to the stressors of the ICU needs more emphasis in the literature, not only because all the possible sources of stress seem to have been enumerated and discussed but because many of the suggestions offered for their reduction avoid the problem, may not be possible, or as Marriot (1975) suggested, have been in use for years.

For this to happen, studies need to be conducted on larger samples of nurses, from broader areas. In the literature only Gentry et al. (1972) have tried quantitatively to assess the psychological responses of nurses to situational stressors in the ICU. Other studies relating to this topic are, as these authors indicated, primarily based on the experience and observations of the author, derived from consulting with, or working on, the unit. Consequently, attention often has been on an anecdotal and qualitative description of the stressors found there. (Huckabay and Jagla [1979] and Jacobson [1978] are important exceptions.) Supporting evidence from questionnaire data, interviews, and contacts with the nurses themselves has been provided less often and relies on relatively small samples, which are usually limited to individual units.

SUMMARY

Stress is a word that is conceptually useful but still lacks the clear delineation necessary for investigation. This is a problem in any nursing research that seeks to define and measure stress and its variables in nurses. Samples too small to validate such a definition are another problem. Yet, it is important that these problems be recognized and the response of the nurse to the environment of the ICU, rather than the "professional situation" alone, be emphasized.

REFERENCES

Bilodeau, C. B. The nurse and her reactions to critical-care nursing. *Heart and Lung,* 1973, *2,* 358-363.

Cassem, N. H., & Hackett, T. P. Stress on the nurse and therapist in the intensive-care unit and the coronary-care unit. *Heart and Lung,* 1975, *4,* 252-259.

Cleland, V. S. The effect of stress on performance. *Nursing Research,* 1965, *14,* 292-298.

Gardam, J. E. D. Nursing stresses in the intensive care unit (letter to the editor). *JAMA,* 1969, *208,* 2337-2338.

Gentry, W. D., Forster, S. B., & Froehling, S. Psychologic response to situational stress in intensive and nonintensive nursing. *Heart and Lung,* 1972, *1,* 793-796.

Hay, D., & Oken, D. The psychological stresses of intensive care nursing. *Psychosomatic Medicine,* 1972, *34,* 109-118.

Holsclaw, P. A. Nursing in high emotional risk areas. *Nursing Forum,* 1965, *4*(4), 36-45.

Huckabay, L. M. D., & Jagla, B. Nurses' stress factors in the intensive care unit. *Journal of nursing Administration,* 1979, *9*(2), 21-26.

Jacobson, S. P. Stressful situations for neonatal intensive care nurses. *American Journal of Maternal Child Nursing,* 1978, *3,* 144-150.

Jones, E. M. Who supports the nurse? *Nursing Outlook,* 1962, *10,* 476-478.

Kornfeld, D. S. Psychiatric problems of an intensive care unit. *Medical Clinics of North America,* 1971, *55,* 1353-1363.

Koumans, A. J. R. Psychiatric consultation in an intensive care unit. *JAMA,* 1965, *194,* 163-167

Lazarus, R. S. Cognitive and coping processes in emotion. In A. Monat & R. S. Lazarus (Eds.), *Stress and coping: An anthology.* New York: Columbia University Press, 1977.

Marriott, H. J. L. Letters to the editors. *Heart and Lung,* 1975, *4,* 802.

Mason, J. W. A re-evaluation of the concept of "non-specificity" in stress theory. *Journal of Psychiatric Research,* 1971, *8,* 323-333.

Mason, J. W. A historical view of the stress field (Pt. 1). *Journal of Human Stress,* 1975, *1*(1), 6-12. (a)

Mason, J. W. A historical view of the stress field (Pt. 2). *Journal of Human Stress,* 1975, *1*(2), 22-36. (b)

Menzies, I. E. P. Nurses under stress. *International Nursing Review,* 1960, 7(6), 9-16.

Michaels, D. R. Too much in need of support to give any? *American Journal of Nursing,* 1971, *71,* 1932-1935.

Selye, H. *The physiology and pathology of exposure to stress.* Montreal: Acta, 1950.

Selye, H. *Stress in health and disease.* Woburn, Mass. Butterworths, 1976.

Simon, N. M., & Whiteley, S. Psychiatric consultation with MICU nurses: The consultation conference as a working group. *Heart and Lung,* 1977, *6,* 497-504.

Strauss, A. The intensive care unit: Its characteristics and social relationships. *Nursing Clinics of North America,* 1968, *3,* 7-15.

Vreeland, R., & Ellis, G. L. Stresses on the nurse in an intensive care unit. *JAMA,* 1969, *208,* 332-334.

Watzlawick, P., Weakland, J. H., & Fisch, R. *Change: Principles of problem formation and problem resolution.* New York: W. W. Norton, 1974.

CHAPTER 6

Perceptions of stress: 1800 nurses tell their stories

Susan M. Steffen

SIGHTS, SOUNDS, AND STRESS OF THE ICU

In approaching the ICU, one is struck by the stark white door, on which the words, "INTENSIVE CARE UNIT—VISITORS ALLOWED 5 MINUTES PER HOUR," are inscribed in red lettering. On entering the unit, one is bombarded with an array of psychosensory stimuli. Initially, the greatest impact may come from what one hears—noises from an endless array of complex machinery. Quickly one's attention is drawn to the psychedelic flashing lights and the maze of people sternly hustling about. Then, one's eyes may focus on those for whom this environment has been created—the critically ill. Patients lie there helplessly with tubes connected to every orifice, looking neither alive nor dead. This is the atmosphere of the ICU. It is difficult to imagine any other environment where the drama of life events is portrayed with such intimacy, intensity, and human emotions.

Yet, amidst all this, it is the ICU nurse who must continually function in this environment, astutely monitoring the patient who has returned from surgery, reassuring the air-hungry emphysemic patient, comforting the family of the dying child, reorienting the confused patient, and assessing the physiological parameters of the patient in an unstable condition.

This description of the ICU may seem overly dramatic. Yet, with careful examination, this seeming overdramatization accurately portrays both the variety and intensity of stresses that the ICU nurse must face in this work environment. Some investigators have suggested that the stresses of the ICU go beyond the adaptive level in both variety and intensity.

How do ICU nurses themselves perceive their work environment? It is now time to learn their story.

OVERVIEW OF THE STRESS MANAGEMENT PROJECT
The need

Initial interest in studying work-related stressors and satisfiers of ICU nurses derived from the nurses themselves, who had returned to the university to prepare themselves for a different nursing role. Bailey and Claus noted that almost one half of some 200 nurses who had enrolled in the Leadership Training Program over the years were former ICU nurses. When questioned about reasons for leaving the ICU, these nurses cited the stress encountered in their work as the most significant factor. Stressors affecting ICU nurses certainly seemed to be an area that warranted further investigation.

Literature search

A review of related studies and articles was conducted. Approximately fifty articles were found that concerned the problem of work-related stressors of ICU nurses. Several studies indicated that the turnover rate among ICU nurses was higher than that of nurses working on other units (Benner, 1975; Razem, 1974). Razem, in a study of nursing attrition in an eastern hospital, reported that critical care units had a 70% turnover rate as opposed to 28% for the rest of the hospital. This study also indicated that ICU nurses left their jobs at a younger age than other nurses and that their length of service was 2 months less than the average length of service in the rest of the hospital. Stressors comprised the major reasons for resigning among this group of nurses. Furthermore, in a survey of over 1000 general hospitals conducted by a major nursing journal, nurses who left the ICU indicated that the stressors of the unit were one reason for their decision to terminate. (Nader, 1972).

The high level of stress in critical care nursing has been documented in a number of articles that were reviewed in the previous chapter. The weaknesses of most of these studies were twofold: (1) The majority of these reports were based on qualitative data gathered by means of observations of a small group of nurses in one particular ICU and (2) the stressors were predetermined by the investigators rather than allowing the ICU nurses to indicate by the use of a "free response" what they perceived the stressors to be.

Preliminary field studies

To further explore the stressors of ICU nursing, Bailey and Claus conducted preliminary studies at several San Francisco sites and in four hospitals in New York and Colorado. Again, ICU nurses and former ICU nurses indicated that high levels of stress in their work environment were significant dissatisfiers or had been a primary factor in their decision to resign from the ICU.

The design

Utilizing the data collected in preliminary studies and the substantiating data from the literature search, Bailey and Claus submitted a proposal to intensify their study of work-related stressors of ICU nurses[1] and to develop training modules for stress reduction. This demonstration training project was approved and funded for a 3-year period, from 1977 to 1980.

The overall design of the Stress Management Project differed from other studies on stress of ICU nurses in the following ways: (1) a broader based sampling of ICU nurses was conducted, totaling approximately 1800, obtained from regional and national samples; (2) the study was designed to elicit stressors as *perceived* by the nurse respondents using a "free-response" question rather than a "forced-response" checklist; and (3) a Stress Management Training Program was developed and implemented, based on the stressors identified by the ICU nurses.

The Stress Management Project was divided into two phases based on the goals and outcome criteria. Phase one involved a survey of ICU nurses concerning sources of stress and satisfaction in ICU nursing. Phase two included the development and implementation of a Stress Management Training Program and evaluation of its effectiveness. This chapter will focus on the phase one efforts.

The questionnaire. A questionnaire was developed to collect information from the ICU nurses. A panel of experts, including intensive care nurses, a psychologist, a nursing educator, and a research specialist, developed the questionnaire and guided it through five rounds of revision. The questionnaire comprised forced-response questions on demographic data and initial attractors to ICU nursing as well as free-response questions on sources of stress and satisfaction in ICU nursing. A pilot study using this questionnaire was conducted in an ICU in southern California prior to its use with the formal sample.

The sample. Initially, the nine-county San Francisco Bay Area was selected as the geographical region for data collection. Eighty-nine ICUs in seventy-four hospitals agreed to participate in this regional survey conducted in fall, 1977. This sample consisted of completed questionnaires from 1238 ICU nurses (60% return rate).

Based on a request from the American Association of Critical Care Nurses (AACN), the sample was increased to include a national survey of members of this organization who were ICU nurses. In the winter of

1978, each of the 191 local AACN chapters was asked to select five ICU nurses randomly from its chapter to participate in the survey. AACN members from 133 chapters across the United States returned completed questionnaires, bringing the national sample to 556 ICU nurses (57% return rate).

Together, the regional and national samples equal a total of 1794 ICU nurses, representing the largest study of ICU nurses that has been reported to date.

Data analysis

The data relative to stressful and satisfying experiences obtained from the nearly 1800 ICU nurses were analyzed by a process called "category formulation" and used by one of the investigators in a previously reported study (Bailey, 1956). The stressful and satisfying experiences that were similar were grouped together. The data were categorized until no new types of stressors or satisfiers were noted. To verify the categorization process, two ICU nurses and a research specialist worked together to objectify the responses and gain group consensus. Through the categorization process the following six major categories of satisfiers emerged: (1) nature of direct patient care, (2) interpersonal relationships, (3) acquisition of knowledge, (4) performance and use of skill, (5) ICU atmosphere, and (6) reward systems. Twenty-nine specific satisfiers were identified and grouped into the six major categories as presented in Table 3. Seven major categories of stressors were identified: (1) interpersonal conflicts, (2) management of the unit, (3) nature of direct patient care, (4) inadequate knowledge and skill, (5) ICU environment, (6) life events, and (7) lack of administrative rewards. Incorporated into the seven major stressor categories were forty-four specific stressors (Table 5).

Further data analysis included computation of response frequencies and percentages for each specific stressor and satisfier. Overall response frequencies and percentages for each major category were then tabulated.

ICU NURSES TELL THEIR STORY
Who are these nurses—a demographic profile

The typical ICU nurse was a 26- to 30-year-old married female with no children. She was a graduate of a diploma school of nursing and was not presently enrolled in school. Although the ICU nurse had been an R.N. for 3 to 5 years, she had worked in only one other critical care unit. She was presently employed in a general ICU or ICU/CCU as a staff nurse and had been employed in that particular unit for 2 years or less.

Nurses tell why they chose ICU nursing

Although a nurse may have many diverse reasons for entering ICU nursing, preliminary studies indicated that ten major reasons were most often cited. When presented with these ten reasons, the nurses were asked to rank order their initial attractors to ICU nursing (Table 1).

Intellectual challenge was seen as one of the top three motivators for choice of ICU nursing among both the regional and national respondents and, in the combined sample, ranked as the number one initial attractor. Nurses believed that the intensity of the patient's illness, along with their own responsibility for his care, required more astute observations, critical thinking, and challenging decision making.

Opportunities for learning was viewed by both the national and regional respondents as one of the top three initial attractors to ICU nursing, being ranked as the second most important initial attractor in the combined national and regional sample. Nurses perceived the ICU as a place to learn about many sophisticated technological developments and as providing an opportunity to implement a wide variety of nursing interventions.

The national respondents saw a patient/nurse ratio of 3:1 or less as an influential factor in attracting them to ICU nursing. The ICU was a place "to be totally responsible for your patients" and to do "total nursing care."

TABLE 1. Initial attractors to ICU nursing–rank order

Regional survey N = 1238	National survey N = 556	Combined regional and national surveys N = 1794
1. Opportunities for learning	1. Patient/nurse ratio of 3:1 or less	1 Intellectual challenge
2. Intellectual challenge	2. Intellectual challenge	2. Opportunities for learning
3. Proficient use of skills	3. Opportunities for learning	3. Patient/nurse ratio of 3:1 or less
4. Learning to handle emergencies	4. Other reasons	4. Proficient use of skills
5. Variety and excitement	5. Variety and excitement	5. Variety and excitement
6. Patient/nurse ratio of 3:1 or less	6. Proficient use of skills	6. Other reasons
7. Being a member of an effective team	7. Being a member of an effective team	7. Learning to handle emergencies
8. Other reasons	8. Recognition and respect	8. Being a member of an effective team
9. Recognition and respect	9. Learning to handle emergencies	9. Recognition and respect
10. Pay differential	10. Pay differential	10. Pay differential

Although this item ranked as the third highest initial attractor in the combined samples, it was a less significant attractor for the regional respondents than for the national respondents.

Proficient use of skills was also a drawing card to the ICU, most notably, for the regional respondents. These nurses felt that technical competence could only be mastered in an environment where numerous skills were constantly performed.

Both the regional and national samples of nurses perceived working on a unit that offered variety and excitement, learning to handle emergencies, being a member of an effective team, receiving recognition, and receiving a pay differential as playing minor roles in initially attracting them to the ICU.

PERCEIVED SATISFACTIONS OF ICU NURSES—BY CATEGORY

What are the major sources of satisfaction for ICU nurses? Nurses in both the regional and national surveys provided a wide variety of responses to this question, ranging from giving direct patient care to working as a member of an effective team to job security. Table 2 presents the rank ordering of the six major satisfiers in ICU nursing, as determined by the regional and national surveys. As noted in the table, the six major satisfiers are (1) nature of direct patient care, (2) interpersonal relationships, (3) acquisition of knowledge, (4) performance and use of skills, (5) ICU atmosphere, and (6) reward systems.

Table 3 provides a rank order of the twenty-nine specifically identified satisfiers grouped within major categories as well as frequency and percentage scores of the six major categories.

TABLE 2. Sources of greatest satisfaction—rank order

Regional survey N = 1238	National survey N = 556	Combined regional and national surveys N = 1794
1. Nature of direct patient care	1. Nature of direct patient care	1. Nature of direct patient care
2. Interpersonal relationships	2. Acquisition of knowledge	2. Interpersonal relationships
3. Performance and use of skills	3. Interpersonal relationships	3. Acquisition of knowledge
4. Acquisition of knowledge	4. Performance and use of skills	4. Performance and use of skills
5. ICU atmosphere	5. ICU atmosphere	5. ICU atmosphere
6. Reward systems	6. Reward systems	6. Reward systems

TABLE 3. Sources of greatest satisfaction

Major satisfiers	Regional survey N = 1238		National survey N = 556		Combined regional and national surveys N = 1794	
	f	%	f	%	f	%
Nature of direct patient care	1563	45.7	771	50.8	2334	48.25
1. Patient improvement, progress, recovery						
2. Close patient contact, patient/ staff ratio, bedside nursing						
3. Patient/nursing care (quality, total, continuity)						
4. Feeling needed, feeling I have contributed, helped						
5. Family contact/support (family or patient and family)						
6. Emotional and/or physical support of patient, critically ill patient (patient only)						
7. Decision making, autonomy, responsibility						
8. Patient/family thanks						
9. Patient/family teaching						
Interpersonal relationships	616	18.0	226	14.9	842	16.45
1. Teamwork ("team")						
2. Recognition, respect, appreciation						
3. People I work with						
4. Working well with others						
5. Staff development, teaching						
Acquisition of knowledge	518	15.2	252	16.6	770	15.90
1. Learning experience, opportunity						
2. Learning techniques, skills, theory (specific)						
3. Intellectual challenge/ stimulation						
4. In-service and continuing education						
Performance and use of skills	528	15.5	177	11.6	705	13.55
1. Use of knowledge and skills						
2. Optimum performance/ accomplishment						
3. Handling emergencies						
4. Satisfactory completion of work						
5. Successfully anticipating situations						

TABLE 3. Sources of greatest satisfaction—cont'd

Major satisfiers	Regional survey N = 1238		National survey N = 556		Combined regional and national surveys N = 1794	
	f	%	f	%	f	%
ICU environment 1. Challenge 2. Variety 3. Excitement, action 4. Pace	165	4.8	90	5.9	255	5.35
Reward systems 1. Pay, benefits 2. Advancement opportunity, charge position	29	0.8	4	0.2	33	.50
TOTAL RESPONSES	3419*	100.0	1520*	100.0	4939	100.0

*Each respondent was given the opportunity to list as many as three satisfiers.

Nature of direct patient care

The responses of ICU nurses strongly indicated that giving direct patient care was the most satisfying aspect of their work, with nearly one half of all the responses related to this activity. The improvement and recovery of patients were the common denominators within this category, as indicated by an Illinois nurse who stated, "Seeing a critically ill 28-year-old automobile accident victim, whose prognosis was grim, get better, leave the unit, and come back to visit really made it all worth while." Heroics were also involved, as this statement from a California nurse indicated: "Pulling that 36-year-old man with three kids and no wife through a cardiac arrest made me feel rewarded and satisfied." Patient improvement became a deep-seated satisfier when the nurse herself felt that she had played a "direct, tangible role" in the patient's progress and recovery, as supported by another account:

She was only 18 years old and had been out riding on her boyfriend's motorcycle. She was described as pretty, bright, and vivacious, but when I met her she was severely bruised, limp, and unconscious. For days I suctioned her trach, checked her vital and neuro signs, and moved her from side to side. Some had given up, but I would not. No one would believe me when I said she turned her head to hear her mother's voice or moved her leg off the pillow. No, it wasn't me dreaming. It really was her voluntary actions. After 2 months she regained consciousness and left the unit. Deep inside, I just knew a lot of it was because of my care.

Although not this dramatic, many nurses related similar types of experiences that really made ICU nursing worth it for them.

The entire spectrum of patient care activities, ranging from direct patient care to support of the family, was identified as an important source of satisfaction, as typified by this response from a New York nurse: "The opportunity to become totally involved with the patient and his family was indeed satisfying." Or the Minnesota R.N. who said, "The opportunity to care for one or two patients and meet all of their needs is what I like about ICU nursing."

Another aspect of patient care that was recognized as a source of satisfaction was the decision-making responsibilities of the ICU nurse. Nurses frequently wrote comments, such as "the challenge of working with a patient and making the right decision" or "the independent active judgments which have direct impact on patients."

The range of responses indicated that ICU nurses really do like patient care. Obviously, the most fulfilling aspect of patient care that was identified was patient improvement and recovery. Realistically, death may occur more frequently than recovery for many ICU patients. Yet, ICU nurses still were able to identify sources of satisfaction other than patient improvement, such as total patient care, family support, and decision-making responsibilities.

Interpersonal relationships

Yes, people at work can make the difference. Interpersonal relationships were identified in the combined regional and national surveys as the second greatest satisfier. "Being part of a skilled team" or the general spirit of teamwork was the most frequently mentioned item. "We all know each other well and work together closely" and "We pride ourselves on teamwork and the ability to function during a crisis" were also frequently voiced ideas.

Nurses stressed the strategic role of recognition and respect as a source of satisfaction in the work environment. The importance of positive feedback from physicians was expressed in this response from on Ohio nurse, "Respect and gratitude from an M.D. for my knowledge and skill in the care of his patients gave me satisfaction." Another nurse shared this comment: "Peer recognition and support really helped me survive in this atmosphere."

Acquisition of knowledge

Overall, acquisition of knowledge ranked third as a source of satisfaction. The following statements typify nurses' responses: "I learn something new every day" and "Continual and never-ending learning is what I find satisfying about ICU nursing."

In addition to the general learning experiences available in the ICU, nurses also appreciated the opportunities to learn specific new skills and to work with new equipment. Gaining technical competence with specialized equipment was widely acclaimed as an immediate and frequent source of satisfaction.

Performance and use of skill

Nurses responded that it was not only "having the knowledge" but really "putting it into action" that served as an important satisfier in their work environments. Some nurses mentioned that the constant opportunity to apply the knowledge and utilize the skills they had learned was fulfilling. Others, more specifically, identified "handling confidently an emergency situation" or "evaluating clinical and lab data and anticipating problems before they occur" as satisfiers. One nurse mentioned, "Getting through a hectic night without any mistakes" as a great source of satisfaction for her.

ICU atmosphere

The ICU atmosphere was "runner-up" for last place as a source of satisfaction. A few nurses described the "highs" from the hectic pace, the constant challenge, and the never-ending excitement of the ICU. Several nurses responded that the variety of patients and the numerous treatment modalities were indirect sources of satisfaction.

Reward systems

A small number of nurses related that the reward systems in the ICU were a source of satisfaction. One nurse stated that she received a pay differential for her specialized knowledge and skill, but most of the nurses did not acknowledge this. A few nurses indicated that they felt secure in their jobs because of the scarcity of qualified ICU nurses and the rapid turnover.

What have we learned? ICU nurses' greatest satisfaction came from giving direct nursing care to critically ill patients. However, significant others in the work environment, such as physicians and nurses, also provided sources of satisfaction, as did the opportunity to gain knowledge and to use skills. The ICU atmosphere and the rewards were looked on as minor sources of satisfaction by the ICU nurses in these surveys.

PERCEIVED STRESSORS OF ICU NURSES—BY CATEGORY

Responses of nearly 1800 ICU nurses relative to what they perceived to be stressful in their work environment indicated almost universal

TABLE 4. Sources of stress—rank order

Regional survey N = 1238	National survey N = 556	Combined regional and national surveys N = 1794
1. Management of the unit	1. Interpersonal conflicts	1. Interpersonal conflicts
2. Interpersonal conflicts	2. Management of the unit	2. Management of the unit
3. Nature of direct patient care	3. Nature of direct patient care	3. Nature of direct patient care
4. Inadequate knowledge and skills	4. Inadequate knowledge and skills	4. Inadequate knowledge and skills
5. Physical work environment	5. Physical work environment	5. Physical work environment
6. Life events	6. Life events	6. Life events
7. Lack of administrative rewards	7. Lack of administrative rewards	7. Lack of administrative rewards

TABLE 5. Sources of greatest stress

Major stressors	Regional survey N = 1238		National survey N = 556		Combined regional and national surveys N = 1794	
	f	%	f	%	f	%
Interpersonal conflicts 1. Medical mismanagement/ disagreement over treatment 2. Staff personality conflicts 3. Unresponsive nursing leadership 4. Hostility, lack of respect from physicians 5. Unavailability of physicians 6. Lack of teamwork, cooperation 7. Communication problems 8. Lack of teamwork with other departments 9. Residents and interns	1041	29.8	1110	31.5	2151	30.65
Management of the unit 1. Inadequate staffing 2. Incompetent staff and floats 3. Lack of time 4. Shifts, scheduling 5. Interruptions—telephone calls, paperwork 6. Patients not needing ICU care 7. Floating out of unit 8. Change of position 9. Lack of continuity in patient assignments	1070	30.7	966	27.4	2036	29.05

TABLE 5. Sources of greatest stress—cont'd

Major stressors	Regional survey N = 1238		National survey N = 556		Combined regional and national surveys N = 1794	
	f	%	f	%	f	%
Nature of direct patient care 1. Emergencies, arrests 2. Unnecessary prolongation of life 3. Critically ill, unstable patients 4. Death and dying of special patients 5. Inability to meet patient's and family's needs 6. Responsibility, decision making 7. Long-term, chronically ill patients 8. Uncooperative patients 9. Routine procedures	890	25.5	843	23.9	1733	24.70
Inadequate knowledge and skill 1. Generalized lack of knowledge 2. Lack of in-service and continuing education 3. Unfamiliarity with equipment 4. Lack of experience and skill 5. Unfamiliar situations 6. Lack of orientation	236	6.7	280	7.9	516	7.30
Physical work environment 1. Lack of, malfunctioning equipment 2. Work space 3. Noise 4. Lack of supplies 5. Too many people 6. Lighting, windows	222	6.4	230	6.5	452	6.45
Life events 1. Personal events 2. Stamina 3. Family	17	0.5	51	1.5	68	1.00
Lack of administrative rewards 1. Inadequate pay, benefits 2. Lack of advancement opportunity	13	0.4	46	1.3	59	0.85
TOTAL RESPONSES	3489*	100.0	3526†	100.0	7015	100.0

*Each respondent was given an opportunity to list as many as three stressors.
†Each respondent was given the opportunity to list as many as fifteen stressors.

agreement among subjects. Although the nurses differed on variables such as age, experience, geographical location, and work setting, they were consistent in their agreement regarding the identification of work-related stressors. This finding has great significance. Not only does a high level of agreement assist in understanding the nature of stress, it also provides reliable data on managing stress. Table 4 provides a rank ordering of the seven major stressors, as determined by the national and regional survey respondents. As noted in the table, the major categories of stressors are (1) interpersonal conflicts, (2) nature of direct patient care, (3) management of the unit, (4) life events, (5) lack of administrative rewards, (6) inadequate knowledge and skill, and (7) physical work environment.

Table 5 presents a rank ordering of the forty-four identified stressors grouped within major categories, with frequency and percentage scores for these seven categories.

Interpersonal conflicts

Interpersonal conflict was identified, in the national survey, as the *major* source of stress of ICU nurses and the *second* most significant source of stress among nurses in the regional survey. When the samples were combined, this category was, overall, the greatest source of stress. Conflicts included nurse-physician problems, nurse-nurse problems, and supervisor-nurse problems.

Nurse-physician problems. Nurse-physician problems were the most intense and frequently cited stressors. Most ICU nurses felt that a collegial relationship rarely existed between nurses and physicians and that physicians neither respected nor listened to nurses' suggestions or opinions. Although these factors in themselves were stressful, the situation became more intense for the ICU nurse when she thought that the physician was either ineffectively or incorrectly managing the patient's condition. A typical comment was voiced by a New Jersey nurse, "Sometimes we know more than the residents and interns, but they're too insecure to listen to us. Other times we're trapped by the archaic methods of the older physicians." Nurses often related experiences where their observations were ignored or their questions unanswered, as demonstrated by the following example.

An 11-year-old girl was admitted to the ICU in septic shock. She was started on dopamine and Isuprel and given large amounts of fluids because of her cardiovascular instability. Several Swan-Ganz lines were attempted unsuccessfully. When the resident came into the room, I informed him that I heard rales in the lung bases bilaterally and the presence of a gallop rhythm. He merely responded, "What do you know—you're just a nurse who thinks she's a cardiologist!"

Nurse-physician problems such as the one just related were frequently identified as major sources of stress. Some nurses spoke of the "double-edged sword," whereby they are blamed if they fail to inform the physician of pertinent facts, but when they do, it is often ignored or they are ridiculed for overstepping the boundaries of their role. The frustration of "being caught in the middle," relative to providing patients with adequate information about their diagnosis or prognosis, was another concern of ICU nurses, as exemplified by the following physician's statement: "Mr. J, you've got a tumor on your lung, but we'll take care of it tomorrow."

Other nurse-physician problems were also identified, such as the incongruity of orders when a number of physicians were attending the same patient or the unavailability of physicians, either because of apathy or poor coverage of the ICU on the evening and night shifts.

Nurse-nurse problems. Nurse-nurse problems represented conflicts among staff nurses of equal rank. The continuously competitive atmosphere, along with the lack of comradery among the rank and file, were viewed as the major sources of stress in the category of interpersonal conflicts. As one Washington nurse stated, "A schism chronically exists—the hard-liners versus the sensitivity seekers, both attempting to prove they're on top. No one ever gets ahead." Most nurses agreed that if the concept of one-upmanship could be remedied without taking away the energy and vitality of the ICU nurse, life in the ICU would be much less stressful.

Nurse-supervisor problems. Some of the very people who might be expected to provide support, the immediate supervisor, be it head nurse or charge nurse, added to the stress of the ICU nurse. The most frequently voiced complaints were the bureaucratic value systems or the inability of the immediate supervisor to provide positive feedback. Read this nurse's reactions to an insensitive supervisor.

I had just finished a hectic night. Mrs. R had arrested twice and each resuscitation took about an hour. And then there was the patient in the other bed. He was terrified, believing this was also going to happen to him. I was able to get everything done and still had some time to talk to him and allay his fears. I left the unit that morning feeling so good, that is, until the head nurse stopped me and informed me that the wastebaskets weren't emptied and the Band-Aids were not restocked.

Instances like this were related continually. Some nurses blamed poor relationships with their supervisors on personality clashes. Other nurses indicated that these stressors were related to "the supervisor being promoted beyond her level of competency." As one nurse stated, "In business, people aren't promoted without management training. Why in the critical care unit, of all places, does this frequently occur?"

It appears that the head nurse cannot be blamed entirely for these conflicts. Many times, head nurses have been used as the scapegoat for more deep-seated problems. As Hay and Oken (1972) suggest, the ICU head nurse is intrinsically in a difficult bind. Although conscientiously fighting for the ICU with nursing administration, the head nurse may be the target of sarcastic comments and indignation from her own staff.

Management of the unit

Management of the unit was identified in the regional sample as the major source of stress and the second most significant source in the national survey. When the samples were combined, this category ranked as the second highest source of stress. This category dealt with nursing management, specifically "those down in the nursing office." A generation gap was felt to exist between "those administrators" and the ICU nurses. Many ICU nurses stated that "*They* are out of touch with reality" or "*They* fail to recognize the physical, emotional, or intellectual demands of the ICU." A wide variety of stresses identified by ICU nurses were blamed on this little-known, often-cited, villain—*the administration.*

Staffing problems. Staffing problems were primarily perceived as stressors caused by the administration. Staffing problems were described as comprising *inadequate* numbers of staff and *incompetent* or poorly trained staff and float nurses. A nurse from California speaks.

One night I was responsible for eight ICU patients. I had another R.N. and an L.V.N. on with me. Then I found out that the R.N. had never been in an ICU and that ventilators frightened her and monitors were foreign machines. Everything went wrong that night. One patient partially eroded his trach, and another patient began bleeding from his aortic graft site. There were phones ringing and physicians yelling orders. I complained to nursing administration; they said things will get better, but they just never do.

This incident, although dramatic in nature, represents what many nurses spoke of individually. The general attitude conveyed was one of lack of concern for the ICU by the nursing administration.

Other stressors. Besides staffing problems there were other stressors. Some responses described the shortages of auxiliary help to do the paperwork, run errands, and answer the phone: "I am expected to change a dressing on a critically ill patient, admit a patient, take blood work down to the lab, and transcribe orders all at the same time."

Stressors such as floating out of the unit, the charge position, and patients not needing ICU care seemed to be much less frustrating to most ICU nurses. Overall, the ICU nurses were willing to tolerate those aspects of their work environment if only the staffing problems were solved.

Nature of direct patient care

Patient care activities represented the third greatest source of stress for the ICU nurse.

Emergencies. Emergencies and the constant potential for crises to occur accounted for the greatest perceived source of stress within this category. A Texas ICU nurse of 6 years described the following stressful situation.

I had just received Mr. M, a coronary artery bypass graft patient, back from surgery. His vital signs were relatively stable and his monitor pattern indicated sinus rhythm with a few PVCs. Suddenly, as I was drawing arterial blood gases, the monitor alarm sounded loudly. "Oh no! It's ventricular fib," I thought. My hands were tremoring, and I felt shaky all over as I threw saline soaks on his chest and reached for the defibrillator paddles.

A multitude of events such as this were related from nurses across the country. The critically ill patient was likened to a "time bomb," with the ever-present potential for an emergency or crisis.

Unnecessary prolongation of life. Unnecessary prolongation of life was a stressor that nurses frequently addressed. Many described anger and frustration, as exemplified by the following response.

A 72-year-old man was admitted to the unit after having been found unconscious in his home. He was placed on a ventilator and was sustained for 5 days, despite three consecutive flat EEGs. I kept questioning why this was happening—why was I spending my time doing this when there were so many patients who really needed my care.

Sometimes the incident was not as well defined. Philosophical and moral dilemmas were viewed by the nurses as making emotional demands on their value system.

It was Christmas Eve. I remember it well. He was a 39-year-old man with end stage cardiac disease. His chest was severely scarred from the many defibrillation attempts due to recurrent ventricular fibrillation. It was only 6 PM, and it had already happened twice on my shift. Then at 6:30 the alarms again sounded. As I was standing over his head with defibrillator paddles charged, he reached out to restrain my hands and gasped, "Please, please let me die in peace." Tears were dripping down my cheeks as I placed the paddles on his chest and heard him moan as the electrical current was transmitted through his body.

Death and dying of special patients. Coping with death and dying was devastating for the ICU nurse, especially when the death involved a patient who was perceived by the nurse as having a good life potential, who was a young child or an infant, or even a patient to whom she had become especially attached.

She was only 7 months old—the daughter of a loving, middle-class family who had mysteriously contracted hepatitis. I took care of her through the course of her illness to the final day, when her abdomen was severely distended and her eyes were swollen shut. I thought I was coping well, yet, when her mother tearfully asked, "How can you stand this?" I broke down. "I've never seen a baby die before." "But you've been a nurse for 10 years," she said quietly. Somehow those 10 years didn't make any difference right then. I left the room severely grief stricken.

Touching accounts such as this were frequently related. Nurses indicated that they often went through a grieving process similar to that of the patient's family. Sometimes, especially in the event of sudden death, it was viewed as a direct affront to the nurse's self-esteem, whereby she questioned her nursing role and, perhaps more importantly, the purpose of work in an ICU.

Other sources of stress. Besides life-and-death stressors, nurses identified other stressors related to direct patient care. There was the constant responsibility for making critical decisions, numerous pain-inflicting procedures, and intense repetitive routine tasks, making the nurse feel like a "hamster on a treadmill."

Contrary to Huckabay and Jagla's finding (1979), ICU nurses in both the regional and national surveys expressed high levels of stress at their inability to meet both the patient's and the family's psychological needs. Nurses were concerned with the lack of time to support families and felt guilty in "being short and abrupt." Some stated that they "had an inner wish to respond but lacked the emotional energy." Others stated that "families were looking for reassurance, but I had no good news to share."

Inadequate knowledge and skills

ICU nurses viewed inadequate knowledge and skills as a considerably less significant source of stress than the three previous categories. Yet, the quantity and variety of complex technical equipment posed tremendous demands on the knowledge base of the ICU nurses. They felt that not only must they know about machines but they also must have a thorough knowledge of illness and an overwhelming amount of information about the signs, symptoms, status of the patient, and skills in carrying out appropriate nursing interventions.

One might expect that the length of time in the ICU or prior critical care experience would comprise factors that would be a common denominator in the category of inadequate knowledge and skills. Contrary to Jacobson's findings (1978), no significant correlation was evident between length of ICU experience and this major stressor category. Nurses with 5 years of ICU experience expressed vague feelings of "not having in-depth knowledge" as often as ICU nurses who were new to the field expressed fear at not knowing how to do certain procedures, such as "draw arterial blood gases." Some expressed fright and awkwardness at having to operate certain equipment, whereas others expressed dismay at the poor orientation or the infrequent staff development classes. Many nurses simply felt overwhelmed at the rapidly advancing technological developments and were concerned with their inability to "keep current."

A common thread that ran through all the responses in this category, whether it was from the new graduate or the seasoned ICU nurse, was the potential feeling of guilt if a mistake was made because of lack of knowledge or skill, as depicted by this response.

He was a lobectomy patient with numerous chest tubes. He seemed fine when I was taking care of him. When I came back the following day, he was intubated because of a tension pneumothorax. Was it me that allowed the chest tubes to kink? Should I have given more thought to the air leak disappearing in the water chamber? I really should know more about chest tubes. I never really have understood them.

Physical work environment

The physical work environment was viewed as a much more minor source of stress by the ICU nurses than might have been predicted. Equipment was not seen as anxiety producing when working correctly but was overwhelmingly stressful when it was not working. Examples of cooling blankets that were heating, ventilators that were supplying inadequate tidal volumes, and infusion pumps that were giving too much fluid were reported as stressful.

The limited amount of work space, especially in units precarved out of existing space, was another source of frustration.

I could not even turn around without the risk of being strangled by the IV tubing or tripped by the numerous cords hanging from various pieces of equipment. I had to crowd under and around machines to do my charting on top of a Gomco suction machine, and then I was bumped by the constant influx of people.

Along with the lack of work space, nurses mentioned the lack of a lounge—"no place to go to escape the hectic pace." Several recounted details of eating lunch at the nurses' station but of quickly losing their appetites.

A few nurses mentioned the sensory overload associated with beeping monitors, swishing suction machines, and hissing oxygen. Most seemed to be so well acclimated to this environmental stressor that they no longer noticed it.

Life events

Few of the ICU nurses tied their personal life events to their work-related stressors. Responses in this category frequently related to overwork at home combined with a hectic work pace in the ICU, as exemplified by this account from an Iowa nurse.

I'm on the run from 6:30 AM, caring for my 5-month-old, 2-year-old, and 4-year-old children. By 2:30 PM I'm exhausted but still have 8 full hours of work to contend with. I am completely exhausted. How can I cope with all these demands and keep up this pace?

Lack of administrative rewards

Only a few nurses identified lack of administrative rewards as a source of stress; however, many nurses responded that few reward systems existed. "We should get a pay differential," was a frequently voiced complaint. More than monetary rewards or benefits, however, the lack of advancement opportunities posed a more serious problem for some California nurses: "Knowing that you will not get promoted for more education or advanced training really gripes me." A frustrated New York nurse expressed well her feelings.

I've worked in this unit for 5 years and feel I've contributed a great deal to patient care, staff teaching, and support to others. Yet, when I applied for a promotion to the next level, I was denied without any explanation. Where do I go from here? Am I forever doomed to the ranks of a "level 2 night nurse"?

What have we learned?

Major stressors for ICU nurses existed in the area of interpersonal conflicts, management of the unit, and patient care activities. Acquiring knowledge to keep up with the trends in ICU nursing and the physical work environment were areas of concern but did not represent the major stressors. ICU nurses viewed their own life events and the lack of rewards as being far less significant sources of stress than might have been predicted.

WHAT DOES ALL THIS MEAN?

This study of nearly 1800 ICU nurses indicates that they do, indeed, have much to say about their work environment. They have shared their initial attractors to ICU nursing as well as their perceived sources of satisfaction and stress. The study findings have numerous implications for nursing education, nursing administration, staff development, ICU middle management, and most importantly, the ICU nurses themselves.

One of the most significant findings is that ICU nurses really like doing direct patient care. They derived their greatest satisfaction from patient care activities. Ways must be provided to reward these nurses for remaining at the bedside as well as opportunities made available for them to learn new and better ways of administering care to the critically ill.

ICU nurses have told the researchers that interpersonal conflicts are the greatest source of stress in their work environment. People, whether physicians, supervisors, or other staff nurses, were consistently perceived as the most common aspect of stress. Methods for dealing with these "people problems" surely need to be explored and solutions found, whether it be through consultative services or other support systems. Perhaps the one common plea heard from many ICU nurses was the need for positive feedback and its potential role in alleviating many interpersonal conflicts.

One final matter in considering the implications of stress and satisfaction for ICU nurses is the intimate relationship between these two aspects of work. As Hans Selye (1976) has emphasized, stress has both positive and negative connotations. In this study, for example, interpersonal conflicts were ranked as the greatest source of stress for ICU nurses; however, interpersonal relationships were cited as the second greatest source of satisfaction. Direct patient care was identified as the most satisfying aspect of work, yet it also was identified as a major source of stress. The nurse's *perception* of a situation as a stressor or satisfier is crucial to any understanding of nursing stress. Changing the nurse's perception by increasing her awareness and enlarging her behavioral repertoire may be the key in turning stressful situations into satisfying experiences. With this enlarged behavioral repertoire from which to draw, the nurse, who previously felt powerless, could then actively control and influence a given situation.

The ICU nurses have told their story. Now it is time to listen, take action, and provide ways for nurses to adapt positively to the many demands in their work environment. This is the charge if the well-being of nurses and those entrusted to their care is to be improved.

NOTE

1. Stress Management Project, Training Grant No. IDIO NU02072, Division of Nursing, National Institutes of Health, Public Health Service, U.S. Department of Health, Education, and Welfare.

REFERENCES

Bailey, J. T. The critical incident technique in identifying behavioral criteria of professional nursing effectiveness. *Nursing Research,* 1956, *5,* 52-64.

Benner, P. Nurses in the intensive care unit. In M. Z. Davis, M. Kramer, & A. L. Strauss, *Nurses in practice: A perspective on work environments.* St. Louis: C. V. Mosby, 1975.

Hay, D., & Oken, D. The psychological stresses of intensive care unit nursing. *Psychosomatic Medicine,* 1972, *34,* 109-118.

Huckabay, L. M., & Jagla, B. Nurses' stress factors in the intensive care unit. *Journal of Nursing Administration,* 1979, *9*(2), 21-26.

Jacobson, S. P. Stressful situations for neonatal intensive care nurses. *American Journal of Maternal Child Nursing,* 1978, *3,* 144-150.

Nader, A. (Ed.). ICU '72: A survey of the intensive care units and coronary care units in 1,111 short-term general hospitals with 100 or more beds. *RN Magazine,* Research Department, Oradell, N.J., 1972.

Razem, J. Nursing turnover in special care units. *Abstracts of Hospital Management Studies,* 1974, *10,* 335.

Selye, H. *Stress in health and disease.* Woburn, Mass.: Butterworths, 1976.

SUGGESTED READINGS

Bilodeau, C. B. The nurse and her reactions to critical-care nursing. *Heart and Lung,* 1973, *2,* 358-363.

Cassem, N. H., & Hackett, T. P. Stress on the nurse and therapist in the intensive-care unit and the coronary-care unit. *Heart and Lung,* 1975, *4,* 252-259.

Eisendrath, S. J., & Dunkel, J. Psychological issues in intensive care unit staff. *Heart and Lung,* 1979, *8,* 751-758.

Gentry, W. D., Foster, S. B., & Froehling, S. Psychologic response to situational stress in intensive and nonintensive nursing. *Heart and Lung,* 1972, *1,* 793-796.

Godfrey, M. A. Job satisfaction . . . or should that be dissatisfaction? How nurses feel about nursing (Pt. 1) *Nursing 78, 8*(4), 89-102.

Godfrey, M. A. Job satisfaction . . . or should that be dissatisfaction? How nurses feel about nursing (Pt. 2) *Nursing 78, 8*(5), 105-120.

Godfrey, M. A. Job satisfaction . . . or should that be dissatisfaction? How nurses feel about nursing (Pt. 3). *Nursing 78, 8*(6), 81-91.

Menzies, I. E. P. Nurses under stress. *International Nursing Review,* 1960, *7*(6), 9-16.

Slavitt, D. B., Stamps, P. L., Piedmont, E. B., & Haase, A. M. B. Nurses' satisfaction with their work situation. *Nursing Research,* 1978, *27,* 114-120.

PART THREE

Strategies for dealing with stress

CHAPTER 7

Taking charge of your stress and well-being

June T. Bailey

During the past few decades nurses have assumed an increasing amount of responsibility for the health care of clients, particularly in the promotion of wellness behavior. Not only are nurses assuming responsibility for wellness behaviors of others but they are also encouraged to promote it in themselves.

The impact of stress on well-being and disease is well documented (Lazarus, 1971; Pelletier, 1977; Selye, 1974, 1977, 1979b). Since stress is often deleterious to well-being, learning to recognize and manage stress effectively is important to nurses, whose work setting and tasks are frequently stress producing and whose pressures and stressors will probably increase in the future.

The purpose of this chapter is to present several ways to recognize stress, to acquaint individuals with methods of dealing with stress, and to review some basic concepts relative to maximizing one's potential for well-being.

DEVELOPING AWARENESS
Self-appraisal

As noted earlier, there are wide individual differences in the perception and interpretation of stress. The amount and intensity of stress that an individual can handle at one time and the overall reaction to various demands and stimuli are different in different individuals.

Learning to live with stress requires getting to know yourself and to recognize what it is that "sets you off." Exploration of self and self-appraisal are key elements in developing awareness.

The following general questions in the self-assessment process might be helpful.
- Is the stress work related?
- Is something going on in my personal life that is worrisome and unfavorable?

• Is it a combination of demands made on me at home and at work?

Knowing the nature of environmental demands can also be facilitated by additional questioning and an information search to determine stress "triggers" and emotional patterns.

• Do I set unrealistic goals and standards for myself that make me anxious?
• Do I resist change because it threatens me?
• Do I feel anxious most of the time?

More detailed behavioral, physical, and emotional indicators, presented in Chapter 3, will also provide cues in developing awareness to one's overall stress reaction patterns. These stress indicators, or messages from one's body, are useful. They alert individuals to the fact that they are pushing themselves beyond a level of healthy functioning, which can result in serious illness.

Self-disclosure

The process of asking for the assistance of others in identifying sources of stress and responses to stress is often helpful. A confidant at work, a friend who is perceived as trustworthy and for whom one has respect, a "significant other," or a family member can add objectivity to the information gathering and appraisal process (Frain & Valiga, 1979). This process is known as self-disclosure and involves revealing perceptions, beliefs, and feelings to others (Jourard, 1971). Studies on the use of the self-disclosure process indicate that individuals who use this process are physically and mentally healthier (Johnson, 1979).

General attitudes and response patterns

Attitudes that one holds toward life in general, as well as attitudes toward work, family members, and colleagues, can influence stress (Mason, 1975). Response patterns of individuals who view the universe as a relatively evil, hostile, threatening environment will be different from those who perceive the world as essentially benevolent and challenging. Generalized attitudes about the world and work are an important factor in appraising and interpreting the many demands and stimuli that surround individuals in their patterns of daily living (Bailey & Claus, 1969). Power resides in each individual in the regulation of thoughts and perceptions. Recognizing that power and taking responsibility for positive attitudes can enrich one's life (Claus & Bailey, 1977; Goldwag, 1979).

The extent to which a positive mental set assists in dealing with environmental demands more effectively might best be illustrated by the example presented in Table 6.

TABLE 6. Response patterns to potential stressor*

Potential stressor (environmental demand—stimuli)	Adaptive pattern	Maladaptive pattern
Change in work schedule From pm to am shift Scheduled to report to work at 6:45 am rather than 2:45 pm	**Thoughts (perception)** "This will be a good day" "I really am looking forward to working the day shift"	**Thoughts (perception)** "I don't have time for breakfast" "Why are *they* always changing my schedule?" "I'll probably get assigned to the trauma patients" "What a life!
	Action Nurse arises at 5 am Prepares and eats nourishing breakfast Bikes to work	**Action** Nurse arises at 6 am Gulps 3 cups of coffee Smokes 4 cigarettes Drives to work Smokes 2 more cigarettes
	Results Arrives at work 10 minutes early Feels relaxed Greeted warmly by head nurse Listens carefully to morning report	**Results** Arrives at work 10 minutes late Couldn't find a parking space Misses morning report Gets "chewed-out" by head nurse for arriving late Worries about "catching-up" and heavy assignment

*Format modified from Farquhar, J. *The American way of life need not be hazardous to your health.* New York: W. W. Norton, 1978, p. 64. With grateful acknowledgment.

As the example indicates, responses to environmental demands can be adaptive or maladaptive. According to Monat and Lazarus (1977, p. 146), the perception of an environmental demand may be judged as "either damaging, threatening, challenging, or conducive to positive well-being."

Through using adaptive patterns of behavior in responding to potential stress or environmental demands, as presented in Table 6, a long-term stress pattern may be avoided.

Identifying levels of stress

Two levels of stress have been described by Pelletier (1977) and Albrecht (1979). These levels are episodic and chronic. Episodic stress is characterized as being of short duration and variable in its intensity.

Chronic stress tends to be continuous without substantial relief, out of voluntary control, and likely to lead to tissue or muscle damage and eventually disease (Benson, 1976).

The Achilles heel

Various systems respond to stress within its physiological domain. Genetically and behaviorally, individuals seem to be predisposed to certain illness. Each person has an inherent weakness relative to wellness behavior, a so-called "Achilles heel." Stress seems to attack whatever system is most vulnerable. For some individuals undergoing stress, the digestive system may be the most vulnerable. A person might experience frequent bouts of indigestion. Other individuals may experience stress in the muscular system, with tightness and discomfort in muscles of the neck or shoulders. Taking note of predispositions to illness can serve as an additional index of one's response to stress.

CAUSAL RELATIONSHIPS BETWEEN STRESS AND DISEASE

It becomes increasingly clear that stress plays an integral role in one's life. Pelletier (1977) reports that 50% to 80% of diseases are stress related. Not only has a causal relationship between stress and disease been proposed by a number of investigators but untoward effects of stress are related to other behavioral problems. Child abuse, marital discord, self-abuse, riots, and violence have been reported as stress-related outcomes (Albrecht, 1979).

Innumerable diseases have been identified as diseases of adaptation. According to Pelletier (1977), Selye (1979a), and others, an ever-increasing number of diseases seem to be associated with stress, some of which are included in the following list:
- Peptic ulcers
- Glaucoma
- Hypertension
- Diabetes
- Arthritis
- Rheumatism
- Allergies
- Cardiovascular diseases
- Mental disorders
- Kidney disorders

Simonton and Matthews-Simonton (1979) propose the existence of a relationship between cancer and stress.

MANAGING STRESS THROUGH SELF-REGULATING MODALITIES

Since the very nature of the practice of nursing is stressful, nurses need skills to unwind and to give their minds and bodies an opportunity to relax. Although there appear to be no magic formulas or simple procedures for stress reduction, a number of mechanisms such as progressive relaxation, meditation, visual imagery, and other self-help methods may be helpful. These methods are alternatives to destructive coping behaviors such as overuse of alcohol, drugs, and other noxious agents.

Role of relaxation exercise

Relaxation exercises are sometimes referred to as "journeys into self" and provide individuals with a mechanism to "unwind." The overall purpose of relaxation meditation is to relieve muscle and mental tension and to induce quieting responses. In effect, these quieting responses allow the body to restore needed energy resources. During stress, high levels of activity in muscle and hormonal systems are activated. Although relaxation exercises and other stress-reducing modalities sometimes afford only temporary solutions to stress, there is evidence that positive results have been obtained in lowering stress levels (Benson, 1976). Meditative techniques and exercises assist individuals to control some of their autonomic functions. This is accomplished through an altered state of consciousness, which produces a mental state of relaxation and fosters temporary healing in a stressed organ system (Benson, 1976). An overview of some of the techniques to combat untoward effects of stress (distress) is presented. However, readers are encouraged to use the training modules presented in the Appendix for more detailed instruction and to experiment with the various self-regulatory modalities to determine what works best in helping them to "unwind."

Relaxation response

The relaxation response is a meditative technique developed by Benson (1976). It is the opposite of the "fight or flight syndrome." The relaxation response consists of relaxing muscles, the use of a mantra such as "one," or other chosen word, and quiet breathing. It involves sitting quietly in a comfortable position, closing one's eyes, and thinking the selected mantra. Essentially the relaxation response is a simplified version of Transcendental Meditation, which was introduced into the Western world during the last decade by Maharishi Mahesh Yogi. However, the relaxation response deemphasizes the ceremonies used by Transcendental Meditation. Those who wish to experiment with the relaxation response are encouraged to follow the instructions presented in Module 3 in the Appendix.

Progressive relaxation

Progressive relaxation is another meditative technique, developed by Jacobson (1978) about 50 years ago, to tense and relax various muscles of the body. This exercise also helps individuals to control muscle tension (see Module 3 in the Appendix for instructions in using this modality).

Autogenic training

Autogenic training is a European technique developed by Shultz and Luther (1959). Autogenic phrases, such as "my feet feel warm", are used to assist individuals to regulate a variety of body systems (see Module 3 in the Appendix).

Biofeedback

Biofeedback uses instrumentation to assist in stress reduction. It is also used as a specific treatment, for example, to lower blood pressure. Kamiya (1968) and Brown (1977) have pioneered this self-regulation technique. Electrical, audiovisual, tactile, thermal, and other sensors are used to change normal involuntary functions of the nervous system to a voluntary control method.

Guided imagery

Guided imagery is a visualization exercise, sometimes known as Meta Imagery, which is simple and effective in eliciting a quieting mental response. The exercise, with which many persons are familiar, entails visualizing a peaceful, private scene that has special meaning to the individual. The individual is encouraged to imagine the sights, sounds, and smells as well as the scene. Guided imagery is used extensively by the Simontons (1979) in their work with cancer patients at the Cancer Counseling and Research Center in Fort Worth, Texas. Spiritual imagery is also used by Jampolsky and Taylor (1979) in treating children with leukemia at the Center of Attitudinal Healing, Tiburon, California.

Aerobic exercise and other physical activities

Releasing tension through exercise is another approach. Aerobic exercises such as jogging, cycling, swimming, skiing, and other bioenergetic modalities have become popular ways to override accumulated muscle tension, which is released through physical activity. A more detailed discussion of aerobic exercise is presented in Chapter 11.

Figure control and muscle-building exercises can also be used to release tension. These exercises are presented in Module 1 in the Appendix.

COPING MECHANISMS IN DEALING WITH STRESS
Coping defined

Lazarus (1971, p. 8) defines coping as "those direct active tendencies aimed at eliminating or minimizing a stressful event which are task and reality oriented." How people cope is a difficult process to study; consequently knowledge about effective coping mechanisms is limited.

Problem solving as a coping process

One of the ways to cope with stress is through problem solving (Lazarus, 1971). Identifying the problem, completing an intensive information search, arriving at a viable solution, and taking action is one way an individual might cope in changing the person-environmental relationship that is stressful. Bailey and Claus (1975) have done considerable work in the area of problem solving and decision making. The ten-step process is presented here as a tool to facilitate the problem-solving, decision-making process for individuals who wish to use problem solving as a method of coping with a stressful environmental demand.[1]

Step one: Define overall needs, purposes, and goals.
Step two: Define the problem.
Step three: Analyze capabilities/constraints and interest groups.
Step four: Specify an approach to problem solving.
Step five: State behavioral objectives and performance criteria.
Step six: Generate alternative solutions.
Step seven: Analyze alternative.
Step eight: Choose the best alternative by decision rules.
Step nine: Implement and control decision action.
Step ten: Evaluate the effectiveness of decision action.

LOWERING THE STRESS LEVEL THROUGH PSYCHOLOGICAL RESPONSES: AN OVERVIEW

There are a number of psychological responses to stress that frequently lower the stress level (McGrath, 1970). A brief review of the more common responses follows.

Disengagement. Disengagment is characterized by a person "giving up." Individuals may feel so threatened and anxious that in a sense they become resigned to the environmental demand.

Avoidance A person may simply repress what is going on and avoid talking about the stress or dealing with it. A common response is, "I don't want to talk about it."

Detachment. A person may insulate himself against threat and remain aloof. This is an intellectual approach.

Denial. Denial is often used by patients who cannot deal with a diagnosis such as cancer. They may deny early symptoms of the disease and thus jeopardize early treatment. It is sometimes referred to as a denial-reaction formation type of thinking and responding.

Other techniques. The judicious use of humor, handling interpersonal relationships, and changing and humanizing the environment are additional ways to lower stress levels. These techniques are addressed in the chapters that follow.

STRESS AND WELL-BEING
Well-being conceptualized

Well-being is conceptualized as a dynamic process in which individuals constantly strive to move toward their highest level of human capabilities and potential in an effort to create a more satisfying and productive life. A key element in the concept of well-being is that individuals need to assume responsibility for their own well-being and strive to move forward on the well-being continuum. In essence, this implies taking responsibility for one's thoughts as well as one's body in an effort to promote well-being and to handle stress (Bates, 1979; Dunn, 1977).

Belloc and Breslow's rules for health

Research on the relationship between health status and stress indicates that establishing and adhering to sound health practices is a highly effective way to deal with stress (Belloc & Breslow, 1972). The major finding of Belloc and Breslow's (1972) 5-year study of 11,000 adults indicated that six simple health habits are associated with longer life. The health habits proposed by these authors include the following practices:

- Eating three meals a day including a nourishing breakfast
- Obtaining 7 to 8 hours of sleep each night
- Moderate drinking
- No smoking
- Maintaining moderate weight

Modules 1 and 2 in the Appendix have more to say about stress and health.

Destructive life-style

In contrast to incorporating good health habits into patterns of living, people are literally killing themselves by self-destructive life-style habits, including the following patterns:
- Drug abuse
- Inadequate nutrition
- Alcohol abuse
- Overweight or underweight
- Lack of exercise
- Lack of adequate rest
- Lack of recreational activities
- Overwork

As the above list indicates, these destructive behaviors are the converse of health habits suggested by Belloc and Breslow (1972).

Dimensions of well-being

Much of Belloc and Breslow's (1972) work on sound health practice is supported by a framework for well-being proposed by Ardell (1979). To integrate one's life-style with dimensions of well-being, Ardell proposes that individuals need to incorporate the following five guidelines into their patterns of daily living:

1. Assume self-responsibility.
2. Develop nutritional awareness and nutritional practices.
3. Maintain physical fitness.
4. Develop a stress management program that works best for you.
5. Develop environmental sensitivity.

In addition to the dimensions of well-being, Ardell (1979, p. 23) presents the following views relative to well-being:

1. High-level wellness is more rewarding than "low-level worseness."
2. A person who practices high-level wellness has greater highs and fewer lows.
3. High-level wellness promotes higher morale.
4. High-level wellness provides individuals with more antibodies to resist illness.

The "bottom line" in stress management: well-being

A book by Pelletier (1977), *Mind as Healer—Mind as Slayer: A Holistic Approach to Preventing Stress Disorders,* offers a number of positive approaches to health, prevention of disease, and the relationship of stress to disease. In essence, the bottom line in the management of stress is summarized by the following statement: "The better shape you're in, the better you can handle stress, and the less likely you are to get stuck in the chronic stress pattern" (Pelletier, 1977, p. 7).

NOTE

1. For more specific information, see Bailey and Claus (1975).

REFERENCES

Albrecht, K. *Stress and the manager.* Englewood Cliffs, N.J.: Prentice-Hall, 1979.

Ardell, D. The nature and implications of high level wellness, or why "normal health" is a rather sorry state of existence. *Health Values: Achieving High Level Wellness,* 1979, *3,* 144-150.

Bailey, J. T. & Claus, K. E. Comparative analysis of the personality structure of nursing students. *Nursing Research,* 1969, *18,* 321-326.

Bailey, J. T., & Claus, K. E. *Decision making in nursing: tools for change.* St. Louis: C. V. Mosby, 1975.

Bates, C. Stress and health: A management approach. *Health Values: Achieving High Level Wellness,* 1979, *3,* 136-143.

Belloc, N., & Breslow, L. Relationship of physical health status and health practices. *Preventive Medicine,* 1972, *1,* 409-421.

Benson, H. *The relaxation response.* New York: W. Morrow, 1976.

Brown, B. *Stress and the art of biofeedback.* New York: Harper & Row, 1977.

Claus, K., & Bailey, J. *Power and influence in health care.* St. Louis: C. V. Mosby, 1977.

Dunn, H. What high level wellness means. *Health Values: Achieving High Level Wellness,* 1977, *1,* 9-16.

Farquhar, J. W. *The American way of life need not be hazardous to your health.* New York: W. W. Norton, 1978.

Frain, M., & Valiga, T. The multiple dimensions of stress. *Topics in Clinical Nursing,* 1979, *1*(1), 43-53.

Goldwag, E., (Ed.) *Inner balance: The power of holistic healing.* Englewood Cliffs, N.J.: Prentice-Hall, 1979.

Jacobson, E. *You must relax* (5th ed.). New York: McGraw-Hill, 1978.

Jampolsky, G., & Taylor, P. Peer healing and self-healing in children. In E. Goldwag (Ed.),

Inner balance: The power of holistic healing. Englewood Cliffs, N.J.: Prentice-Hall, 1979.

Johnson, M. Anxiety/stress and the effects on disclosure between nurses and patients. *Advances in Nursing Science,* 1979, *1*(4), 1.

Jourard, S. *The transparent self.* New York: Van Nostrand-Reinhold, 1971.

Kamiya, H. Conscious control of brain waves. *Psychology Today,* 1968, *1,* 57-60.

Lazarus, R. S. The concepts of stress and disease. In L. Levi (Ed.), *Society, stress, and disease* (vol. 1). London: Oxford University Press, 1971.

Mason, J. A historical view of the stress field (Pt. 2). *Journal of Human Stress,* 1975, *1*(2), 22-36.

McGrath, J. *Social and psychological factors in stress.* New York: Holt, Rinehart & Winston, 1970.

Monat, A., & Lazarus, R. S. *Stress and coping: an anthology.* New York: Columbia University Press, 1977.

Pelletier, K. *Mind as healer: Mind as slayer.* New York: Delacorte, 1977.

Selye, H. *Stress without distress.* New York: J. B. Lippincott, 1974.

Selye, H. A code for coping with stress. *Association of Operating Room Nurses, Inc. Journal,* 1977, *25* (1), 35-42.

Selye, H. *The stress of my life* (2nd ed.). New York: Van Nostrand-Reinhold, 1979. (a)

Selye, H. Stress: The basis of illness. In E. Goldwag (Ed.), *Inner balance: The power of holistic healing.* Englewood Cliffs, N.J.: Prentice-Hall, 1979. (b).

Shultz, J., & Luther, W. *Autogenic training: A psychologic approach in psychotherapy.* New York: Grune & Stratton, 1959.

Simonton, O., & Matthews-Simonton, S. Stress, self-regulation, and cancer. In E. Goldwag (Ed.), *Inner balance: The power of holistic healing.* Englewood Cliffs, N. J.: Prentice-Hall, 1979.

CHAPTER 8

Dealing with people problems

Ann Baldwin

A nurse-physician problem

The ICU head nurse arrives at work to find the surgical resident and midnight charge nurse by her office door. Each angrily describes the other's poor judgment and clinical shortsightedness. They disagree over treatment for a patient's fungal pneumonia.

A head nurse–staff nurse behavior problem

Staff meetings on the medical floor are reported to be tense. Predictably, a few staff are ridiculed for their lateness, dress at work, or neatness. The target of this "hot-seating" is rotated among all the staff.

A nurse-nurse personality pattern problem

The nurses in a busy ICU are split into two camps: the tough aggressives and the gentle supporters. Both groups fear and are angry at each other. Each group wants the other to change to become more like "us."

A head nurse–staff nurse ethical problem

Two new night nurses in the emergency room have reported to work several nights in a row smelling of beer. When the young charge nurse speaks to them, they become angry. The next day, the head nurse also raises the issue with them. Later they are overheard complaining bitterly to other staff about administrative injustice.

These four vignettes are examples, rather extreme ones, of actual interpersonal relationship (IPR) problems in acute care settings. Luckily, IPR problems of this magnitude are not a daily event in an acute care unit, but they are common and distressing.

This chapter will address the following aspects of IPR in acute care settings: (1) scope of IPR problems, (2) causes for IPR problems, and (3) interventions to (a) prevent IPR problems, (b) solve problems as they occur, and (c) deal with blowups and severe tensions.

SCOPE OF IPR PROBLEMS

The recent nursing and acute care literature supports the importance of interpersonal relationships in acute care settings. In a national survey of members of the American Association of Critical Care Nurses, Claus and Bailey (1979) found that interpersonal relationships were the second most common source of perceived stress for nurses, identified by 30% of the nurses. In a similar survey of ICU nurses in the San Francisco Bay Area, Bailey and Claus (in progress) found IPR problems to be a large source of satisfaction for nurses as well.

In Huckabay and Jagla's (1979) study of ICU nursing stressors in six hospitals in the Los Angeles area, interpersonal communication ranked second to patient care as a perceived stress factor. Horvath (1979), too, found interpersonal conflict an important element to study in a thoracic-cardiovascular ICU.

Jacobson (1978, p. 150) studied neonatal ICUs: "A striking feature of the nurses' reports was their almost total emphasis on psychosocial conflicts". Youngner, Jackson, and Allen (1979, p. 35) studied physicians and nurses in a newly opened medical ICU to determine "the basis for conflict and tension surrounding decision making in ICU settings".

CAUSES FOR IPR PROBLEMS IN ACUTE CARE SETTINGS

The major cause for IPR problems is people. When two or more people interact, they often perceive events or problems differently and use different behavior mechanisms to solve problems. In addition, they bring to the interaction their own unique characteristics and experience. These differences between people are fertile grounds for interpersonal problems.

Should these statements leave the reader wishing for solo practice in nursing, it is important to note that nursing practice always involves other people—patients, families, and co-workers. Even if the impossible "people-less" condition existed, the lone nurse would soon discover tension and conflict *intra*-personally.

Since other people are a reality in current nursing practice, what is it about the nature of acute care environments that makes IPR problems so salient? Four factors appear to intensify IPR problems there: (1) pressures to focus on clinical tasks, (2) fast pace of the work, (3) general frustration level, and (4) barriers to communication.

Focus on clinical tasks

The pressures to focus single-mindedly on clinical tasks contribute to IPR problems. In one ICU the nurse caring for Mr. X was concerned about his unexplained diarrhea. Her trips to the linen closet were increasingly rushed. Twice she bumped into co-workers without apology or comment. At lunch, staff complained about her "rudeness."

To maintain health, groups (and individuals) need a balance between emotionality and work (Stack & Thelen, 1963). Acute care settings that try to focus exclusively on clinical tasks are subject to periodic blowups and tension releases, which serve to restore temporary emotional balance. Later, I shall present arguments for providing regularly scheduled discussions to examine group emotionality before great tensions have a chance to build.

The need for acute care staff to focus on clinical tasks is understandable. Their mission is often a crucial, life-and-death matter for patients and families about whom the staff care as people. Furthermore, they perform these important tasks in the context of limited time, limited supplies, and limited staff. No wonder their attention is repeatedly pulled to clinical tasks.

Fast pace

A second factor that also intensifies IPR problems in acute care settings is the fast pace. This sometimes necessary, fast pace accentuates a strong, constant belief in time urgency—that minutes and seconds count every hour, all day, every day, until retirement. In some research on type A and B behavior, this sense of time urgency is associated with impatience with other people, hostility, and irritability (Friedman & Roseman, 1974). Thus a fast work pace can contribute to a semi-permanent belief that time is urgent, which leads to impatience and hostility with other people.

General frustration level

Gentry, Foster, and Froehling (1972) have documented considerable situational hostility (resentment, irritability, verbal aggression) in acute care nurses in two hospitals. It arises from the enormous work demands, not from nurses' personalities (Gentry et al., 1972; Menzies, 1960). (See Chapter 5 for alternative arguments about situational as opposed to personality contributors to nursing stress.) This general frustration level in acute care settings contributes to the interpersonal difficulties that occur.

Several factors intensify the general frustration level in acute care settings. The high standards for saving life and promoting full patient functioning stimulate a herculean effort from staff. The frequent reality is that these standards are impossible to meet: Not all lives can be saved, and many patients return to partial functioning, at best. This decrepancy between goal and outcome often leaves the staff frustrated and irritable.

The common, sometimes daily, event of death in acute care units is a frustration to the staff. A cross-cultural study of grief and mourning (Rosenblatt, Walsh, & Jackson, 1976) has demonstrated that death provokes frustration, anger, and aggression in the survivors. It often falls to ritual specialists (clergy, health care professionals) to help survivors deal with this irritability. The task is profoundly difficult when health professionals themselves experience deep frustration and anger at the patient's death. The position of being survivors and ritual specialists simultaneously also contributes to considerable frustration and irritability.

The combination of other issues in acute care work, such as low pay, inadequate physical working environment, overtime work, and shift rotation, produces irritable and frustrated acute care staff (Tasto, Colligan, Skjei, & Polly, 1978). Is it any wonder, then, that they experience interpersonal friction?

Barriers to communication

Acute care settings come with built-in geographical, temporal, and social barriers to adequate interpersonal communication. In some ICUs without central monitoring, staff are assigned to one patient room. Their communication is with a float nurse or with the unit clerk by speaking over the intercom. In other settings, staff are assigned to opposite ends of the hall and rarely see one another.

Temporal barriers block communication as well. Staff meetings can never include all the staff because some must always cover the patients. The rapid turnover of nursing staff (33% to 63% annually in one cross-regional United States study, McCloskey, 1974) and rapid rotations of medical staff (sometimes monthly) prevent relationship development among co-workers.

Social factors, too, contribute to blocked interpersonal communications. Some argue that gender role differences between nurses and physicians are the primary cause of IPR conflict (Nadelson, 1976; Rosini, Howell, Todreo, & Dorman, 1974). Youngner et al. (1979) posited that professional background differences have more effect on this conflict than gender. Another difference that influences communication relates to the concepts of teamwork among disciplines as opposed to the traditional authority hierarchy (Youngner et al., 1979). Ambiguity about which of these models operates in a setting seriously hampers interpersonal communication.

INTERVENTIONS FOR IPR PROBLEMS

The first step in changing interpersonal problems in acute care settings is an awareness that these problems exist. Horvath (1979) found that nurses in a thoracic-cardiovascular ICU were more likely to be aware of this conflict than physicians. Youngner et al. (1979) urged open acknowledgment that these IPR problems exist in the acute care unit.

The second step is for unit staff to adopt some beliefs supportive to

IPR change. Staff need to believe that (1) it is possible to improve IPR problems in this unit, (2) it is a good use of work time to address IPR problems, and (3) unit staff themselves have to change the interpersonal climate.

In my experience, acute care units often balk at this step. Many staff believe that adults cannot change their interpersonal behavior ("no one can change his personality, you know"). Some also believe that such attention to interpersonal difficulties is a distraction from clinical tasks, which are regarded as "the real work." In addition, most staff (indeed, most human beings) hope that the head nurse, the medical director, or the "troublemakers" will solve the problem for them. Unfortunately, these false beliefs serve to perpetuate IPR problems and the nurse's sense of powerlessness at work.

The third step in dealing with IPR problems involves choosing and implementing the appropriate intervention. Before some possible interventions are examined the assumptions underlying them will be presented. These assumptions are that (1) there will always be some IPR problems when two or more people work together; (2) these IPR problems will require approximately the same amount of time, whether prevented, solved as they appear, or solved when they are major crises; and (3) acute care staff resist efforts to solve IPR problems because such problems appear frightening evidenced by avoidance and lateness to meetings where IPR issues are to be discussed and claims that such discussions are a waste of time.

Interventions to prevent IPR problems

The purpose of interventions at this preventive level is to head off as many IPR problems as possible, which can be accomplished by (1) spending time together, (2) aiming for unity among unit leadership, and (3) providing psychological support services.

Staff in an acute care unit need opportunities to spend structured time together, for example, at monthly staff meetings and patient care conferences. In one acute care unit, nursing staff invited physicians to their weekly Kardex rounds, where patient problems were discussed. Physicians grew to value this contact opportunity. These staff gatherings "allow one individual or group to view and understand the struggles, attitudes, and ambivalence of another" (Youngner et al., 1979, p. 39). They allow acute care staff to clarify how each sees the goals of the unit (teaching, research, service) and their personal goals for working there, thus increasing chances that the staff will share at least some goals in common.

In addition to structured time together, staff need opportunities to relax and play together. In several ICUs with which I am familiar, the staff go bowling regularly (at 7:30 AM!), take tap dancing lessons together, and sponsor disco parties. In other units the staff come to work 30 minutes early for coffee and relaxed conversation. These contacts help the staff see their co-corkers as persons and diminish the sense of strangeness of talking only to an intercom.

A powerful intervention to head off IPR problems is unity between the medical and nursing heads of the acute care unit. The quality of their relationship sets a tone for physician-nurse relationships in the unit. The aim of such unity is shared goals for the unit and mutual respect. Although this intervention is powerful and important, it is *very* rare because it is difficult to accomplish. Unusual foresight and maturity are required from these discipline leaders.

Another intervention with preventive potential is psychological support services for acute care staff. Regular, sanctioned opportunities can be provided to discuss the pressures and stresses of acute care help to release some of the IPR steam and friction. These group and one-to-one discussions on the work site underscore the reality that acute care work is difficult for everyone. It helps to cut through the myth that "only the weak can't take the heat." (See Chapter 10 concerning the role of the nurse consultant.)

Interventions to solve problems as soon as they occur

Interventions at this level aim to deal quickly and effectively with IPR problems in acute care units. Even in units with a zestful, caring interpersonal climate, IPR problems will appear. Many of these problems require the use of conflict resolution skills. Kramer and Schmalenberg (1977) have provided an excellent model of conflict resolution for nurses. It includes the following principles: (1) mutual willingness to resolve the conflict, (2) balance of power between the conflicting parties, (3) movement to agreement concerning shared goals, (4) full exploration of the conflict issue, (5) solutions that meet the needs of all conflicting parties, and (6) ongoing evaluation of solutions. These conflict resolution skills are useful for nursing and medical staff at all levels, but especially for managers who are called on daily to mediate interstaff conflicts.

Another important intervention is the use of a strategy from organizational psychology called team development (or team building). During team development the consultant (1) uses interviews or questionnaires to learn the staff's perceptions of problems and (2) conducts an off-site meeting to discuss and plan remedies for the identified problems. "The objective of team development is the removal of immediate barriers to group effectiveness and the development of self-sufficiency in managing group process and problems in the future" (Beer, 1976, p. 956). Follow-up contacts are frequently necessary. These consultants need to be skilled and are usually paid for their services.

Interventions to deal with blowups or severe tensions

When IPR problems reach the severe level, interventions must be of the "big gun" variety and often require an outside consultant to help with team building. Such a consultant needs to be a conflict negotiator with considerable power and skill. These consultants are hard to find when one needs them. Other interventions that can help ease the pressures of severe blowups include having the tense parties avoid one another, agreeing to disagree about the issue at stake, agreeing to a demilitarized zone around the conflicted issue, and arranging for transfers or resignations of involved parties.

All interventions for this level of an IPR problem are costly in money, work effectiveness, and professional esteem. Solving as many problems as possible before they reach this severe level costs more in courage but less in all other resources.

SUMMARY

This chapter has explored a common problem in acute care settings—that of interpersonal relationships. It has addressed the prevalence and causes for IPR problems in acute care units. In addition, it has suggested interventions to prevent IPR problems, to solve the problems quickly, and to deal with severe IPR tensions. The chapter suggests that some IPR problems are inevitable but that many can be modified by early, regular attention to this important aspect of work in acute care.

REFERENCES

Bailey, J. T., & Claus, K. E. Summary of a study of stress in intensive care nursing in northern California, U.S. Department of Health, Education, and Welfare (NIH Grant No. 1-D 10-Nu02072), 1978.

Beer, M. The technology of organizational development. In M. Dunnette (Ed.), *Handbook of industrial and organizational psychology*. Chicago: Rand McNally, 1976.

Claus, K. E., & Bailey, J. T. A study of stress in intensive care nursing: Regional and national results. Unpublished paper, 1979.

Friedman, M., & Rosenman, R. *Type A behavior and your heart*. New York: Alfred A. Knopf, 1974.

Gentry, W., Foster, S., & Froehling, S. Psychologic response to situational stress in intensive and nonintensive nursing. *Heart and Lung*, 1972, *1*, 793-796.

Horvath, P. Nurse-physician perceptions of ICU nurses' role. *American Journal of Nursing*, 1979, *79*, 917.

Huckabay, L., & Jagla, B. Nurses' stress factors in the intensive care unit. *Journal of Nursing Administration*, 1979, *9*(2), 21-26.

Jacobson, S. Stressful situations for neonatal intensive care nurses. *American Journal of Maternal Child Nursing*, 1978, *3*, 144-150.

Kramer, M., & Schmalenberg, C. *Path to biculturalism*. Wakefield, Mass.: Nursing Resources, 1977.

McCloskey, J. Influence of rewards and incentives on staff nurse turnover rate. *Nursing Research,* 1974, *23,* 239-247.

Menzies, I. E. P. Nurses under stress. *International Nursing Review,* 1960, *7*(6), 9-16.

Nadelson, T. Psychiatrist in the surgical intensive care unit: A consideration of staff roles. *Archives of Surgery,* 1976, *111,* 118-119.

Rosenblatt, P., Walsh, R., & Jackson, D. *Grief and mourning in cross-cultural perspective.* Boston, HRAF Press, 1976.

Rosini, L., Howell, M., Todreo, I., & Dorman, J. Group meetings in a pediatric intensive care unit, *Pediatrics,* 1974, *53,* 371-374.

Stack, D., & Thelen, H. Emotional dynamics and group culture. In M. Rosenbaum & M. Berger, (Eds.), *Group psychotherapy and group function.* New York: Basic Books, 1963.

Tasto, D., Colligan, M., Skjei, E., & Polly, S. Health consequences of shift work. Technical report for National Institute for Occupational Safety and Health. Washington, D.C.: U.S. Government Printing Office, 1978.

Youngner, S., Jackson, D., & Allen, M. Staff attitudes towards the care of the critically ill in the medical intensive care unit. *Critical Care Medicine,* 1979, *7*(2), 35-40.

CHAPTER 9

Humanizing the health care environment

Pamela Baj

There's many a life
of sweet content
whose virtue is environment.

Walter Learned

IMPACT OF THE WORK ENVIRONMENT

The delivery of health care does not take place in a vacuum. The interpersonal transactions that transpire among health providers and clients occur in a physical, social setting. Most persons have a general notion about the nature of the environment, or at least what it should be: restful, convenient, aesthetically pleasing, and generally supportive. Surprising as it may seem, only recently has attention been directed to the impact of the work environment and other variables on the nurse. As was noted in Chapter 6, the regional and national surveys recently conducted by Claus and Bailey indicated that elements in the work environment such as malfunctioning equipment, crowded unit space, noise, poor lighting, poor ventilation, and other variables were indeed perceived by nurses as stressors.

Historically, the effects of the working environment on the nurse-provider are not without serious precedent. In 1788 in a typical Parisian hospital, the annual death rate of patients was 25%, whereas the death rate of the attendants ranged from 6% to 12% (Burling, Sentz, & Wilson, 1956). It was more than a cliché that the attendants who lived outside the hospital were much healthier than those who lived within it.

Today's hospitals are much more than simple brick and mortar. They are complex sociological, technological, biological, and psychological systems that produce powerful stimuli that affect the lives of both patients and providers. Florence Nightingale recognized the link between hy-

79

giene and health, and Pasteur drew attention to techniques of asepsis. Health providers are now free of the occupational epidemics that ravaged early hospital staffs, but they cannot escape the impact of the work setting on their physical and emotional lives.

Suppose one were to survey nurses and ask them to visualize and describe an ideal physical setting for health care. The environment would probably be described in terms such as "restful," "supportive," "inviting," "healing," and other positive phrases. Few, if any, would admit that they had spontaneously described their own hospital work environment. Should they be asked to do so, comments would be made such as "very crowded," "underlighted," "awkwardly arranged," "dirty," "drab," "noisy," "smelly," and many other unfavorable reactions to surroundings that are an assault to the senses of the people who work there.

Clearly a great deal more is known now about the impact of environment on people than in 1788. However, when one sees some of the "modern" working conditions of today's nurses, one wonders. The observations extend not only to nurses' stations but to the hospital environment as a whole—hallways, reception areas, lounges, treatment rooms, operating suites, kitchens, locker rooms, patient care units, and other areas. The discrepancies between what already exists in today's hospital working environments and what could be provided in terms of positive work environment stimuli are merely a question of applying careful analysis and known principles to the problem. But what are the parameters of the environmental problem, and what can be done to humanize the environment? These are the questions that need to be addressed.

PERCEPTION: RELATING TO THE ENVIRONMENT

The relationship of the individual to the environment is described as a problem of perception. Perception has been defined as the way a person relates to the environment (Claus & Claus, 1971). It also encompasses the physical phenomena of sensations and their integration at a cognitive level, particularly when discussion is restricted to human beings. Individuals perceive the real world through their senses of sight, touch, smell, and hearing. Each of these senses, in turn, can evoke powerful emotional stimuli. Yet, the mind is not a passive agent. When confronted by strong stimuli, the organism adapts or copes. It is the reaction to these stimuli, the biological response to stimuli, that creates problems for the nurse. What are these stimuli? What are some of the reactions that they provoke? How can they be modified to obtain the desired biological and emotional outcome? These are provocative and timely questions which call for action.

COLOR AND LIGHT: TAMING THE RAINBOW

One of the most powerful stimuli in the environment comes from visual images that people perceive. The modern hospital is an overwhelming visual experience. Sight is a complex, behavioral, intellectual function that is largely learned and subject to cultural influence. Two broad characteristics are used to describe the visual physical world: form and color.

Use of color

Color can be described in biological terms as the complex action of the electromagnetic spectrum on the central nervous system by means of the eye. The powers of discrimination of the human eye with respect to color are awesome. It is estimated that "the human has the ability to discriminate seven and a half million different colors using a language having very few color names" (Triandis, 1964). Yet the colors are capable of producing different biological responses in a given individual. Gerard (as reported by Birren, 1969) established that the color red produced sustained increases in blood pressure, autonomic sweating, blinking, increased respiration, and a somewhat higher anxiety level in some patients. The color blue tended to produce the opposite effects. It has been proposed that many of the psychological responses to color are culturally dependent and learned responses. Although white has been a traditional marriage color in American culture, and is yet associated with positive feeling, in India white is the color of burial shrouds and mourning. Thus in different cultural settings the color may provoke different emotional responses.

Although architects and designers have recognized for some time that either "warm" or "cool" colors can be selected to meet functional and aesthetic needs, working areas of the hospital often leave choice of colors to someone's personal whim without regard for basic principles or needs. It appears that the color needs of nurses in a surgical intensive care unit, where the emotional stimulation is high pitched, are not the same as those of nurses in a medical unit who are caring for chronically ill patients. The nurse whose pace and activities are accelerated in the ICU does not need the added overstimulation of "warm" or "hot" visual colors. This fast-paced setting could benefit from "cool" hues, less intense and lower value colors. Primary hues blended with white, black, or other colors to mute their intensity would provide a low-keyed background of visual stimulation. Colors such as rust, peach, beige, and ivory are good examples. By contrast hallways, nursing stations, or staff lounge areas in a chronic medical ward need the added stimulation that color can provide. Here one can take greater liberty with warm colors such as reds, oranges, bright yellows, or vivid greens. Intensity and purity of color tones can be much higher, and contrasts can be used with greater effect. The stimulation can be absorbed by the staff because of the slower pace and more moderate stimuli.

Use of light

Light itself is a variable to be considered in the working environment. Often the light is designed with purely functional demands in mind. True enough, the staff must have sufficient candlepower and low-level glare to deal with the amount of visual work required on the job. However, too little attention is being given to the quality of the light in terms of the psychological impact on the staff. When the light in a working environment is considered, a clear understanding of one general principle in lighting and color perception should be remembered. For colors to appear natural and normal to the human eye, the following conditions of lighting should prevail: (1) at low levels of light intensity, the light should be of a warm hue, that is, tend to the pink and yellow tones; and (2) at high levels of light intensity the light should be cool in hue, that is, tend toward the blue-white specturm (Kruithof, 1941).

To envision this principle in action, consider the typical intimate lighting in a first-class restaurant. With a low level of lighting, usually candlelight, the light casts a rose or yellow-pink hue, which flatters the features of its patrons and gives them a healthy appearance. In contrast, the produce sections of most supermarkets use a high-intensity fluorescent light source that, with its blue-white quality and high output, enhances the sharp color of the produce and maximizes its attractiveness. To illustrate what happens when this principle is broken, simply picture what the faces around you look like when illuminated by the blue-white lights of a large parking lot that are some distance away from you. The colors all around you seem washed out and unreal. This finding leads one to ask: "How does this apply to the working environment?"

Picture the night staff nurse who has dutifully turned off all the hallway lights in patient areas and who now has, as her sole working light, a small, goose-neck fluorescent lamp over the medicine closet. The result is that the colors and objects around take on a washed-out, dreary appearance. There is no visual relief from the dim blue-white light. Visual tedium is added to the monotony of decreased noise. The effect is one of general sensory deprivation, a condition well known to be associated with sluggish reflexes, wandering attention, and occasionally impaired judgment (Selye, 1976). A more humane, aesthetic approach would use low-level incandescent lighting and would highlight pictures, work areas, traffic pathways in the hall, and other areas. All this could be done without interfering with patient comfort. In addition, it would provide maximal normal color stimulation for someone struggling with the tedium of a long night shift.

An area of neglect in most hospital environments is the provision of lounges for the staff. These areas should serve as temporary respites from heavy demands of the professional nurse's schedule. They should be an environmental oasis, providing a haven of comfort and relaxation to break the monotony of constant high-level or low-level stimulation and illumination. Yet how many nurses' lounges are lit with the same unflattering (and cheap) fluorescent lighting found in the work areas. If an overworked nurse needs a visual confirmation of how demanding her job is physically, she need only step into the nurses' lounge of many hospitals, where associates can reflect and comment on her sallow complexion, the crow's-feet around her tired eyes, and the wrinkles in her brow. However, it may be the light that makes the nurse look old and as if unable to sustain the load. Areas where relaxation and the psychological feeling of well-being are important deserve careful consideration of lighting. The subtle impact is not to be underestimated; nor should the need continue to be unmet.

NOISE: THE UNSEEN POLLUTION

Although no one thinks of hospitals as noisy places, some of the traditional quiet associated with the hospital environment that was characteristic 50 years ago has been lost. Indeed, it is ironic to see traffic signs such as "Hospital Zone: Quiet" on the street corner when bedlam reigns inside. What are the parameters of noise that can affect the nurse in a modern hospital environment?

Several investigators have determined that the average person finds auditory stimulation to be objectionable when the noise level reaches 37 decibels, at which point the level is capable of interfering with reception of conversational speech (Kryter, 1970). The sleeping patient can perceive noise at almost all levels normally heard while awake, but sleep patterns begin to be disturbed when the level reaches about 27 decibels. One survey found that about 60% of all patients at discharge complained about hospital noise levels when questioned directly (Smook, 1966). Relative to noise and the staff nurse, some areas of the hospital may be psychologically hazardous from the standpoint of noise; that is, the nurse is exposed to disrupting, nonpurposeful auditory stimulation which interferes with purposeful activity.

A recent survey found the average *minimum* noise level of a university teaching hospital intensive care and coronary care unit to be in excess of 60 decibels (Turner, King, & Craddock, 1975). This was the *minimum* level of sound, usually around 4 AM. The maximum levels frequently approached 90 decibels, particularly from 1 to 7 PM. The type of noise was not specifically examined, but those familiar with ICUs would readily admit to a bombardment of sound—electrocardiograph monitor beeps, that recurrent gurgle of aspirators, the click and sighs of the respirators, the steady chirps of IVAC units, the constant ringing of telephones, the squawk of paging beepers, the running of water, the flushing of toilets, the staccato of chest percussion, and many, many others. Most of these noises are informationally neutral sounds, although they may interfere with staff activity. If one adds to this background rumble the occasional plaintive moan, distressed cry, anxious command, desperate plea, or sudden scream, one can appreciate the subjective reality of 90 decibels of sound.

The constant exposure to this stimulus is inherently stressful to both nurses and patients and should be minimized to provide optimal delivery of care and recovery. Again the implications for the staff are clear. Noise should be minimized in work areas. Lounge areas should be acoustically separate from the work area to provide needed relief. Conversely, night staff nurses on medical floors may need some auditory variation in the long silences of their shifts. Experimentation could be undertaken to provide the night staff with some stimulation such as low-level music or perhaps some form of "white sound" stimulation, defined as low-level, subjectively nonimportant sound. This can be a recording of rain, waves, or wind played at low level and was originally designed to help insomniacs. These sources of low-level stimulation have important arousal value (Selye, 1976). Apparently, the cortical activating centers of the brain need some low-level stimulation to prevent the onset of sensory deprivation syndrome. Low-level white sound can perform this function, allowing the person to maintain attention span and minimize wandering of thoughts. Lessening of generalized muscle rigidity and slower autonomic function have also been noted. Investigations that apply these findings to the nurse's work environment are needed. Clearly sound has an important part to play in the long-term adaptive responses of the professional nurse.

SMELL: THE ANCESTRAL RESPONSE

The olfactory sense is a part of the environmental perception that is seldom considered in discussions of the work setting. Smell is the perception of molecules that stimulate the nasal mucosa and, in turn, the first cranial nerves. These nerves eventually tie into the limbic system, a portion of the brain contained in the areas concerned with arousal and emotion. There is some evidence to suggest that this area of central nervous system function is a teleological holdover from earlier Darwinian stages of human development. Certainly in lower animals, including primates, smell is a strong initiator of certain behavior patterns. Recently, understanding of pheromones, the volatile short-chain fatty acids elaborated by modified apocrine glands, has shed light on the initiation of patterns of mating among primates (Morris, 1967). It has been suggested that the use of perfumes and artificial scents by humans is a subconscious imitation of suppression of a similar system. Clearly, smells can evoke strong behavior patterns in lower animals. Since humans have assumed a higher level of complex development, dependency on these mechanisms is no longer needed, since such actions are usually initiated on a conscious cortical level. However, subtle evocative pressures may remain as vestigial elements of early biological evolution in humans.

The hospital provides many smells to which the nurse is constantly exposed. Some smells are obviously repugnant, such as the esters of fecal material, the bilious odor of vomitus, and the acrid smell of melena. Other smells may subconsciously tug at the emotions of nurses in unsuspecting ways. The faint sweet smells of ketoacidosis, the musty smell of uremia, the faint traces of inhalation anesthetics, the overpowering astringent smells of antiseptic cleaning solutions, the friendly smell of starched linen, and even the occasional whiff of flowers brought in by visitors—all are sensations that at times can be overwhelming.

It is safe to say that most hospitals are immoderate in the amount of olfactory stimulation provided to staff and patient alike. Clearly there is a need to rethink problems such as adequacy of airflow through working areas, sources of air ventilation, regulation of ambient temperature and relative humidity, frequency of total turnover of the air, and air maneuverability. In practical terms, relevant questions are posed, such as, "When an offensive odor develops, must the whole wing suffer for hours until natural oxidation removes the offending molecules from the air?" or "Can the air be quickly and quietly vented and resupplied with fresh, clean air that has been raised to the proper temperature and humidity?" Like too many other aspects of the hospital environment, the air quality frequently resembles the conditions prevailing in the eighteenth century.

MICROBES: THE BIOLOGICAL HAZARD

Although sensory stimuli impact on the nurses' responses to their environment, more subtle hazards exist that may have a profound effect. From the earliest days of the hospital, microbial infection has been a critical problem in the hospital environment, which frequently places nurses at risk in their care-giving roles. When Pasteur introduced the concept of asepsis to modern medicine, he made it possible for patients with pathological organisms to be grouped together within the confines of a hospital so that infection precautions could be taken.

However, despite present-day infectious control procedures, health providers should not be deluded by the current antibiotic armamentarium and then ignore the potential hazards of the sea of pathogenic microbes that arise in the daily course of duty. Viruses are the single major hazard nowadays. Principally the hepatitis viruses represent a constant hazard to the medical community at large. Some nurses, such as those working in hemodialysis, are at the higher risk than others. Anyone who comes into contact with blood, blood products, or products from any point in the gastrointestinal tract is risking infection. Viruses transmitted by way of respiratory droplets such as adenovirue, ECHO viruses, varicella, and enteroviruses represent potential hazards for health providers. Bacteria, particularly *Staphylococcus aureus* and hemolytic strains of *Streptococcus, Neisseria meningococcus,* the pneumonic strains of plague, also can be acquired through contact with infected patients.

The nurse who does not maintain a vigilant attitude toward these unseen agents cannot reasonably expect to avoid them. Well-known interventions include frequent handwashing; gowns, masks, and gloves when appropriate; prompt attention to cuts and minor abrasions on the skin; avoidance of extreme fatigue; insistence on proper ventilation; and utilization of health care preventive maintenance programs provided by the employer (Jenny, 1976). Although the hospital often is perceived as a "clean" and "sanitary" environment, the army of microbes gets daily reinforcement from new patients and opportunistic infection of established patients. Avoidance of this biological cycle is mandatory for nurses if they are to maintain their well-being.

RADIATION AND PARTICLES: THE HAZARDS OF ENERGY

The agents of radiation and particles are neither perceived nor are they biological. They represent forms of energy that may be hazardous to health professionals who are exposed to them in certain circumstances. Radiation may be encountered as part of the diagnostic or therapeutic armamentarium of the hospital. Radiation hazards exist principally as gamma radiation, a form of electromagnetic energy that is capable of penetrating most surfaces without difficulty, including the skin. This energy force has the capability of inflicting severe damage to living cells. Radiation is encountered in the hospital from diagnostic x-ray equipment; from therapeutic radiation equipment that can be either supervoltage x-ray, cesium, and cobalt isotope machines; or from therapeutic isotope implants. Each of these poses a biological hazard for the nurse who works around them or comes into contact with patients who are encountering them as part of their care. Radiation energy damage is dose dependent, and the dose depends on time of exposure and distance from the sources. Practically speaking, it behooves all nurses to minimize both time and distance exposure to radiation sources of all kinds as much as possible. If nurses must work around these radiation sources, the following precautions should be taken:(1) use proper shielding such as lead aprons and gloves; (2) watch for spills and contamination of articles by the patient; and (3) stay away from the diagnostic and therapeutic beams as much as possible. Radiation is the invisible part of the work environment that can be a threat to the nurse's well-being (Luckmann & Sorensen, 1974).

Another form of energy that may become increasingly important in an understanding of the impact of working environments is the "ion effect," which refers to a phenomenon involving charged particles in the air (Soyka, 1977). The theory proposes that in many environments the air becomes depleted of negatively charged ions, that is, the Santa Ana winds of southern California, the foehn winds of southern Germany and Switzerland, and man-made environments exemplified in poorly ventilated and recirculating air conditioning systems. The depletion of negative ions may lead to general malaise, deterioration in mental functions, and various effects on the autonomic systems. When negative ions are restored to the air by rain, ocean spray, or waterfalls, the general effect produces a state of mental alertness and increased energy. Proponents of ion effect theory claim that many man-made environments, including hospital systems, are literally ion depleted, and thus in jeopardy. Devices to generate negative ions are sold in Europe and the Soviet Union, but regulations in the United States and Canada forbid them to be promoted as anything but "air cleaners" (Soyka, 1977). Research into the controversial area of ion effect continues, but the day may come when nurses will need to monitor the relative concentration of negatively charged particles in the air for their own well-being and that of their patients. Adjustment of the relative concentrations of ions will be as simple as adjusting the thermostat. Clearly, humans are entering aspects of environmental control undreamed of in earlier times.

ROLE OF THE NURSE MANAGER

Previous discussions of environmental aspects suggest the need for a coordinated approach to the problem of the nurses' work environment. It should become the responsibility of the nurse manager to identify and deal with aspects of the working environment that need to be changed. A primary consideration of the work environment is the conceptualization of working space. The need for personal and professional space demands that the form and function of the physical plant carefully follow the needs of the people who will use it, predominantly the nursing staff (Grubbs & Short, 1979). The use of space will depend heavily on the quality and quantity of personal interactions among the users (Altman, 1975). Ideally, the nurse administrator will be involved in the primary planning of the work environment. Assessment tools, such as the Moos Environment Scale (Insel & Moos, 1972) can be used to evaluate the nurses' perception of the work environment, particularly if the instrument is used to determine both the nurses' perception of the actual work environment as well as the nurses' perceptions of what it should be. The discrepancy between "what is" and "what should be" will provide the nurse manager with information about needed changes in the work environment.

Professional help from architects, lighting engineers, and health care facility planners can be used to outline modifications or improvements to bring the environment into line with projected ideals (Goodwin, 1979). It is the responsibility of the nurse administrator to (1) provide peripheral input such as alerting the staff to the phenomenon of environmental stress; (2) facilitate ongoing maintenance, replacement of physical facilities, or both; (3) provide adequate staffing patterns to enable nurses to take periodic breaks from their work; and (4) provide support service to the staff to enable them to deal more effectively with the environmental stresses as well as with other stressors and dissatisfiers (Goldstein, 1979). Nurse managers must not only deepen their awareness relative to the impact of the environment on patients and health providers but, more importantly, they need to take action and facilitate change.

SUMMARY: THE CHALLENGE FOR THE FUTURE

This chapter has discussed how perceived factors in the environment such as light, color, sound, and smell impact on the nurses and on others. In addition, attention has focused on unperceived factors, such as microbial, electromagnetic, and molecular elements that affect the nurse. Recognizing, changing, and controlling these environmental factors (when possible), are crucial in providing a safe, supportive, humanistic health care environment for the well-being of nurses, other health providers, and recipients of health care.

REFERENCES

Altman, I. *The environment and social behavior*. Monterey, Calif.: Brooks/Cole, 1975.

Birren, F. *Light, color, and environment*. New York: Reinhold, 1969.

Burling, T., Sentz, E., & Wilson, R. *The give and take in hospitals*. New York: G. P. Putnam, 1956.

Claus, R. J., and Claus, K. E. *Visual environment: Sight, sign, and by-law*. Don Mills, Ontario: Collier Macmillan, 1971.

Goldstein, J., Nursing station design using a social theory model. *Journal of Nursing Administration*, 1979, 9(4), 21-25.

Goodwin, I., A guide to planning critical care units. *Journal of Nursing Administration*, 1979, 9(6), 20-25.

Grubbs, J., & Short, S., Nursing input to nursing unit design. *Journal of Nursing Administration*, 1979, 9(5), 25-30.

Insel, P., & Moos, R. The work environment inventory, Social Ecology Laboratory, Department of Psychiatry, Stanford University, Palo Alto, Calif., 1972.

Jenny, J. What you should be doing about infection control. *Nursing 76*, 1976, 6, 78-79.

Kruithof, A. A., Tubular fluorescent lamps. *Philips Technical Review*. March, 1941.

Kryter, K. D. *The effects of noise on man*. New York: Academic Press, 1970.

Luckmann, J., & Sorensen, K. *Medical-surgical nursing: A psychophysiologic approach*. Philadelphia: W. B. Saunders, 1974.

Morris, D. *The naked ape*. New York: McGraw-Hill, 1967.

Selye, H. *Stress in health and disease*. Woburn, Mass.: Butterworths, 1976.

Smook, I. Who complains about noise in the hospital? *RN* 1966, 29, 94-98.

Soyka, F. *The ion effect*. New York: Bantam Books, 1977.

Triandis, H. C. Cultural influences upon cognitive processes. In L. Berkowits (Ed.), *Advances in experimental social psychology* (Vol. 1). New York: Academic Press, 1964.

Turner, A. G., King, C. H., & Craddock, J. G. Measuring and reducing noise. *Hospitals*, 1975, 49(15), 85-86; 88; 90.

SUGGESTED READINGS

Davis, M., Kramer, M., & Strauss, A. (Eds.). *Nurse in practice: A perspective on work environment*. St. Louis: C. V. Mosby, 1975.

Garfield, C. (Ed.). *Stress and survival*. St. Louis: C. V. Mosby, 1979.

Lazarus, R. S., & Cohen, J. B. Environmental stress. In I. Altman & J. Wohlwill (Eds.), *Human behavior and the environment: Current theory and research* (Vol. 1), 1977.

McLean, A. (Ed.). *Occupational stress*. Springfield, Ill.: Charles C Thomas, 1974.

CHAPTER 10

Providing consultative services

Ann Baldwin

Various approaches to reduce stress in health professionals have been described in the literature. Indeed, the subject of job-related stress and how to cope with it is an ever-increasing topic in the news media and professional journals. One approach that appears to hold promise in reducing the stressors of acute care nurses is through the use of a nurse consultant. The role of the nurse consultant is frequently classified in job descriptions as nurse facilitator, liaison nurse, psychiatric or mental health nurse, or other titles. Although each of these titles has a somewhat different meaning, there is a commonality in the overall purpose—to reduce stress for patients, families, or staff.

Nelson and Schilke (1976) have traced the evolution of one of these roles, that of psychiatric liaison nursing. They credit Johnson (1963) with the first description of the cross-service nursing consultative role. These early nurse-to-nurse consultations were one or two meeting discussions about a particular patient problem. Later, they became more extensive, that is, ongoing consultative relationships, which included direct assessment of, and interventions with, patients and families and consultation with nursing staff.

The recent nursing literature shows growing interest in these stress-reduction roles (Garrant, 1977; Kolson, 1976; Przepiorka & Bender, 1977; Shubin, 1979; Simon & Whiteley, 1977). What is missing from this literature, however, is information to aid staff and administrators of acute care settings in deciding (1) whether to develop a stress-reduction role, (2) what type of role, (3) for which parts of the acute care setting, (4) for what time period, and (5) with what outcome criteria. The focus of this chapter is to explore these assessment, intervention, and evaluation issues in the choice of a nurse consultant to reduce stress in acute care settings.

OVERVIEW OF STRESS-REDUCTION ROLES

Stress-reduction roles have been aimed at two populations: patient/family and nursing staff. Robinson (1974) has described those patient and family contacts frequently found in mental health liaison nursing. The liaison nurse receives a referral from nursing or medical staff concerning patients or family members who are having difficulty with their illness and hospitalization or are displaying behavioral problems. The liaison nurse then interviews the patient and relevant caregivers and makes an assessment that is used in collaborative care planning with caregivers and the patient and family (see also Roberts, 1976).

Depending on patient and caregiver needs and abilities, the liaison nurse may also be active in interventions with the patient and family. Often, these interventions are one or two crisis intervention sessions aimed at reducing extreme anxiety and helping patients reestablish effective levels of functioning. Occasionally, the liaison nurse contracts for longer interventions with patients and families, for example, a series of discussions to help a badly frightened wife of a patient with intractable cardiac arrhythmias.

Another significant population with whom nurse consultants work is the nursing staff. The literature describes different purposes and formats for these contacts, the most common of which is a group meeting with nursing staff and the nurse consultant. This meeting is described in a variety of ways: (1) consultation conference (Simon & Whiteley, 1977); (2) group discussion (Roberts, 1976); or (3) problem-solving conference (Przepiorka & Bender, 1977). These sessions comprise weekly or bimonthly meetings of the available nursing staff, held in conference rooms on the unit or, occasionally, away from the work setting. The topics include work-related issues of mutual interest to group members. Meetings last for 30 to 60 minutes.

Some consultants also provide opportunities for individual discussions with nursing staff (Simon & Whiteley, 1977). These individual contacts allow frank discussion of issues that nursing staff want kept confidential or are not of mutual interest to the entire nursing group (e.g., conflict over an evaluation). Common topics in these one-to-one meetings include reactions to a difficult death, overload from too many burdens at work and at home, and moderate to severe interpersonal conflicts.

Other formats that are used occasionally include meetings with middle and top managers of nursing service, which often focus on staff conflicts, discipline issues, and program planning (Cooper, 1976). A valuable, but rarely used, format is a joint meeting between nurses and physicians on an acute care unit. Youngner, Jackson, and Allen (1979) recommend such regular meetings to allow the two disciplines an understanding of each other's concerns and views. A recent nurse-physician session dealt with the staff's difficulty in treating a 27-year-old man with

his second myocardial infarction *as a patient*. This was especially difficult, since the patient also had been a popular physician on the cardiology
service. Nurses and physicians shared how difficult this situation was
from each of their perspectives.

In addition to the format, the purposes of the nurse consultant's contacts with staff are important. Like the format, they can vary. The most
common purposes are to (1) improve clinical problem solving, (2) improve the interpersonal work climate, and (3) provide psychosocial learning opportunities (e.g., information about crisis intervention or stress reactions). Other, less frequently stated, purposes include resolution of
interpersonal conflicts and discussion of bioethical dilemmas (Davis,
1979).

Some purposes for these staff contacts are not stated, but they are
nonetheless real. These consultant-staff contacts provide opportunities to
(1) discharge tensions ("empty the frustration bag from working here,"
Di Mars, 1979); (2) receive emotional support from peers; (3) enhance
the sense of group membership with peers; and (4) decrease the sense of
aloneness and inadequacy in working in an acute care setting. In summary, most consultant-staff contacts are multiple purpose; that is, they
focus simultaneously on problem solving, interpersonal work climate,
and emotional support.

ASSESSMENT FOR APPROPRIATE INTERVENTION

Many of the possible stress-reduction interventions that acute care
settings can use have been just described. How would the staff or manager of an acute care unit decide which of these activities (if any) would
be effective on the unit? The decision should include three elements: (1)
problem-solving process to locate appropriate interventions, (2) flexibility
in intervention choice; and (3) evolution of future interventions.

The problem-solving process starts with the felt need expressed by
nursing staff or managers for some intervention or help. Stress-reduction
procedures are inappropriate when there is no felt need among health
professionals.

When a need is felt, however, it is important to transform the need
into a goal. This movement from "felt need" to "goal" involves identifying
what has caused the need. For example, in one acute care unit there was
considerable conflict between the head nurse and the staff. Staff had
regular meetings with a psychiatrist, who believed that meetings should
focus on patients, not staff. The staff from the unit felt a need to discuss
their relationship problems with the head nurse to resolve the intense
conflict among them.

Their solution was to approach the nursing consultation service for help in effecting this conflict resolution. The nurse consultant and the psychiatrist decided to meet jointly with the staff to discuss this interstaff conflict.

This example illustrates the persistence needed to address a felt need. At first the staff were not successful in convincing the psychiatrist to discuss the interstaff conflict and had to go outside to the nursing consultation service to get legitimation for their felt need and help in addressing it. Also illustrated here is the flexibility and colleagueship of the psychiatrist in agreeing to the changed goal. (Nurse consultants should take note and follow this example.)

The goal in this example was resolution of a staff conflict. Other common goals include providing better psychosocial care to patients, developing skills with difficult patients, and developing a more supportive atmosphere with nursing and medical co-workers.

Once the staff and nurse manager have identified the need and goal, they are in a position to find appropriate interventions to address it. For example, in a busy ICU with no central monitoring, staff often were suspicious and critical of one another. They needed to find ways to decrease this suspicion. Since one of the contributors to the suspicion was the staff's infrequent, pressured contacts with one another, the goal was to provide regular, interstaff contact. In this ICU, group meetings were preferable to individual contacts with nursing staff.

On the other hand, when the felt need concerns only a few staff (e.g., several nurses disciplined for coming to work late), the intervention might be limited to the disciplined nurses, head nurse, and nurse consultant. A meeting to plan the confrontation and resolution session is another intervention that would involve only the head nurse and nurse consultant. From several possible appropriate interventions, the nursing staff and the nurse consultant choose the one most likely to be productive.

Having followed a problem-solving process from felt need to intervention of choice, the nursing staff, manager, and consultant are ready to proceed. On many units weekly consultation conference meetings are chosen to address the goals of improved psychosocial care to patients and regular, staff contact opportunities.

Nursing staff, managers, and consultants need to remain flexible in the face of requests for other services. For example, when the consultant and staff trust each other sufficiently, staff will occasionally ask for one-to-one consultation about personal reactions to work issues, friends with psychiatric problems, and referrals for counseling. Staff also may strongly suggest that the consultant see a patient—usually to validate the staff's perceptions. These requests, although incidental to the main intervention, are almost always reasonable and important to honor, if at all possible. These services can strengthen the nursing staff in the performance of their work role and are legitimate concerns and requests.

Likewise, the consultant occasionally may ask for flexibility from the nursing group, for example, that the group shelve a patient problem so that they can address an important loss, such as the sudden resignation of the head nurse. Mutual flexibility and trust from consultant and nursing staff and crucial to their continued working together.

Over a period of time, nursing staff and the consultant may discover new ways of working together. Simon and Whiteley (1977) describe a consultation conference that moved from short psychosocial lectures and patient topics chosen in advance to topics chosen spontaneously in the conference. Other consultant-nursing staff groups may explore additional ways to work effectively together, such as (1) using on-the-spot intervention rather than group discussions at a later time, (2) employing one-to-one discussions as a lead-in to group discussion, and (3) planning to have a short period of regular group discussions followed by discussions only when the staff requests them, for example, crisis contact. In Kolson's (1976) study of nurses' expectations of consultation conferences, 71% of nurses preferred this crisis contact model. Consultants, on the other hand, usually prefer steady work.

Consultants and nursing staff may discover that certain topic areas require different formats. For example, a difficult death may require one-to-one contacts before group discussions are appropriate, whereas conflict resolution may require a highly structured meeting and consultant outreach to the participants afterwards.

ASSESSMENT FOR APPROPRIATE ACUTE CARE UNIT

How can nursing staff, managers, and consultants decide if a particular nursing unit is likely to benefit from stress-reduction interventions? The following four criteria are often useful in assessing the situation: (1) a felt need, (2) shared self-esteem among nursing staff, (3) willingness to change, and (4) administrative support.

The unit nursing staff and managers must feel a need for change, for something different and better. In the absence of this felt dissatisfaction, stress-reduction strategies are better used on other units or not at all.

Paradoxically, the unit also needs to feel considerable satisfaction with its past and present performance. This shared professional self-esteem in nursing staff and managers is the positive base that supports changes in functioning. It also allows staff members to examine the parts of their clinical and work group functioning that they want to improve. Only people who like themselves can look at their behaviors.

Furthermore, nursing staff and managers need to be willing to change things. It is hard to look at one's unit and not see perfection; it takes courage. Deciding to change some of the problems is even harder and needs persistent effort. Staff and managers should agree to put energy into planned change for as long as it takes to improve the problem. This point in the assessment process is a crucial one. It is where most potential stress-reduction interventions stop or at least are delayed until the unit personnel decide that change is worthwhile.

A last area to assess is the administrative support for the stress-reduction intervention. The head nurse's willingness and active support are crucial. Reluctant support from the head nurse greatly restricts the chance for success. In many acute care units, support from the medical director is also crucial. Some units develop effective stress-reduction interventions with only token support from the medical director; when that person actively opposes the intervention, however, the failure potential increases. In units where the head nurse is reluctant or the medical director actively opposed, it is better to postpone or cancel stress-reduction interventions.

Related to administrative support is support from other persons influential in the acute care unit. Simon and Whiteley (1977) credit a respected physician with low-key encouragement to the nursing staff's development of a consultation conference. In my experience, other influential supporters have been former head nurses of the acute care unit, assistant directors of nursing, nursing staff who have participated in other group discussions, and unit social workers.

TIMING ISSUES IN INTERVENTION

After assessing an appropriate intervention for an appropriate care unit, a number of issues arise about the timing of stress-reduction interventions. The beginning of the intervention should follow as quickly as possible the assessment procedure. The unit staff are usually motivated, somewhat uncomfortable, and ready to get started. Consultation conferences sometimes fail because of long delays, such as a month or more, in getting started. For example, in one stressed oncology service, one fourth of the staff resigned or went on sick leave during that delay.

Another important issue is how often to schedule the intervention. In Kolson's survey (1976) of the University of Minnesota Hospital's medical-surgical nurses, 71% preferred consultation when problems arose, rather than on a routine basis. Przepiorka and Bender (1977, p. 756) speak well for nurse consultants' views about timing:

> Exclusive use of the crisis model is discouraged. It is hoped that through regular meetings with a consultant, the nursing staff will build their psychosocial skills, will be better able to handle crises when they arise, and will develop a more preventive orientation.

This common conflict between nurse consultants and unit nursing staff must be negotiated by them. Their mutual resolution needs to consider the time commitments of each and the goals of the intervention. For units that want to meet regularly, weekly or bimonthly meetings allow for the most consistency and mutual trust development.

Cooper (1976) states that the consultant's role is to work herself out of a job, hypothesizing that nursing staff eventually achieve their goals for the stress-reduction intervention and will terminate the contract. In reality, staff turnover in acute care settings often prevents such goal achievement. Termination more often comes from dissatisfaction with the intervention or the nurse consultant rather than from goal accomplishment, which indicates the need for regular evaluations of the intervention. Facing this evaluation and possible termination is productive for the work functioning of all the participants.

CHOICE OF THE APPROPRIATE CONSULTANT

The chapter has operated on a number of assumptions about the consultant who carries out the stress-reduction interventions. These assumptions need to be made explicit. The consultant is *not* the formal supervisor of the acute care unit, is employed outside the unit, is a nurse, and is from a mental health or behavioral science background. These assumptions should be examined, since some effective consultant–nursing staff relationship *do not meet* them.

The literature is divided in advocating stress-reduction roles by the formal supervisor or by a nonsupervising consultant. Hay and Oken (1972) recommend regular group meetings with someone outside the unit's administrative hierarchy. This nonsupervisor can participate as a professional colleague, peer, and ally in the nursing staff's work stresses.

Others recommend use of the unit's formal leaders. Kornfeld (1971) and Cassem and Hackett (1975) recommend discussions with the medical director. Holsclaw (1965) and Jones (1962) urge group leadership by the head nurse of the acute care unit.

Acute care units choose wisely which of these leadership patterns will work best for them. Some group discussions thrive under administrative leadership, whereas others wither. The nursing staff usually know best.

The consultant can be a unit administrator or not or from inside or outside the unit staff. Hay and Oken (1972) recommend the outsider, who provides more anonymity and fewer sanctions against talking openly about work stresses. Acute care units sometimes choose a trustworthy insider. One surgical ICU drafted a skilled, nurturing surgical nurse clinician to lead their stress-reduction group. Another ICU strongly maintained that they could not trust an outsider as much as several unit nursing leaders. Again, nursing staff usually know best about what will work for them.

Another assumption is that the consultant must be a nurse. Przepiorka and Bender (1977) describe such a nurse–nurse consultation service. One advantage of their model is to lower suspicion about discipline differences. Others describe flourishing group discussions where the leader's different discipline had no negative effects (Hay & Oken, 1972; Koumans, 1965; Simon & Whiteley, 1977). A third model is co-leadership by a nurse and a psychiatrist, which facilitates productive discussion of the nurse-physician conflicts in acute care settings (Hay & Oken, 1972; Przepiorka & Bender, 1977). Acute care units often have a good sense of which of these models will work best for them.

Psychiatric and mental health personnel are frequently used in these consultant roles. Hay and Oken (1972) contend that such psychological sophistication allows the consultant not to overdo the self-exploration parts of stress reduction. Holsclaw (1965) supports psychologically trained consultants. Conversely, as reported earlier, some nonpsychiatric personnel provide excellent leadership for stress-reduction groups. In addition, some consultants such as Bilodeau (1973) have both psychiatric and acute care skills.

The specific skills, attributes, and attitudes of the consultant are more important than position in the unit, discipline, or clinical background. Important consultant skills include group leadership, counseling (one-to-one and group), teaching, and consultation. In most cases, consultants have acquired these necessary skills in a graduate program in nursing, psychiatry, psychology, or social work. Several personal attributes also are important, such as patience, tolerance of anxiety and other emotions (especially the sadness arising from work with extremely sick patients), and tolerance of differences. Very importantly, consultants need to be serious about becoming worthy of trust from acute care staff. For example, consultants should be careful about confidences shared with them, clear about their areas of competence, aware of their own imperfections, and willing to repair damage when they make a mistake.

The effective consultant needs to possess a philosophy which includes a belief that working on an acute care unit is valuable, that acute care units are worth the stress of working there, that mastering the stresses of working on an acute care unit is possible, and that the staff on this acute care unit provide good nursing care. These attitudes help strengthen the collegial relationship between the consultant and nursing staff.

Clearly, no consultant possesses all of these skills, attributes, and attitudes, nor is the ideal acute care unit anywhere to be found. However, looking for these qualities in a consultant should maximize successful outcomes from stress-reduction interventions.

EVALUATION OF STRESS-REDUCTION INTERVENTIONS

Evaluative research on the effects of stress-reduction interventions in acute care units has been minimal. Deloughery, Neuman, and Gebbie (1970) measured the effects of mental health consultation on nurses' problem-solving ability. The study, which was the only one using nurses, found mixed effects from the consultation. Nevertheless, the researchers contributed concepts and instruments sorely needed for research in this difficult area, such as measures of group problem solving.

Mannino (1975) has reviewed thirty-five studies of mental health consultation in the human services and found that 69% showed a positive change. When change was measured in different target groups, the percentage of positive effects varied somewhat: 74% in nurses, 58% in patients, and 50% in the system (acute care unit or hospital). Overall, these studies show that one type of stress-reduction intervention, that of mental health consultation, has a positive effect on care in human service organizations.

To improve consultation effectiveness and to justify use of resources for these stress-reduction interventions, such outcome studies should continue. In the meantime, acute care units and consultants need criteria against which to judge outcomes. An important criterion measure in evaluating effectiveness is satisfaction: "How satisfied are the participants and the unit administrators with the interventions?" Another criterion measure is goal attainment: "Is the unit achieving its goals for the intervention (improved psychosocial care or warmer working environment)?" A final measure addresses staff participation: "How readily do staff participate in the intervention?"

Later, studies need to consider more comprehensive criteria, such as clinical problem solving, job satisfaction, staff turnover, interpersonal climate, staff learning and development, and conflict resolution skills. In addition, numerous patient and family outcomes need measurement, including acute stress reactions, ICU delirium, confidence in the health care team, speed of recovery, amount of residual psychological disability, and family attachment and functioning after the hospitalization.

Another level of evaluation that may be difficult to measure is the ethical effect of the stress-reduction intervention. For example, the question needs to be answered: Is this consultation conference draining frustration that would otherwise be used to change an exploitive situation? If consultant or unit staff believe this to be so, the intervention should stop or be changed to alter the exploitation. In another ethical consideration, consultant and unit staff need to decide: Are the goals of this intervention and of this acute care unit consistent with the participant's personal value system? For example, if one values patient and family autonomy in choosing the length and type of medical treatment, if would be inconsistent and ethically improper to be a consultant, or staff nurse, in an acute care unit where such patient autonomy was not practiced (e.g., some research units).

SUMMARY

This chapter has examined a variety of stress-reduction roles used in acute care settings. Literature support and clinical examples have been used to assist staff and administrators to make the following decisions:

1. Is there a need to develop a stress-reduction role?
2. What type of consultant role should be selected?
3. Which units of the acute care setting should be selected to participate?
4. What is the time frame for the stress-reduction program?
5. What are the outcome criteria?

Many programs and interventions to reduce stress in acute care settings have been successful and well received by nursing staff. Evaluative research supports the use of such programs to enhance work effectiveness. Interested managers and nursing staff are encouraged to develop such stress-reduction programs for their settings.

SUGGESTED ACTIVITIES

1. Determine if your unit has had a support group or consultation group. Why did it start? Who participated? Who led it? Was it helpful? Why did it end?
2. Determine if other units in your hospital or geographical area have such groups. What are they like? Are they helpful?
3. If you are interested in having such a group on your unit:
   a. Approach your head nurse.
   b. Define clearly the purpose and type of group you would like.

    c. Remind yourself that you will have to explain actively your situation to any consultant you choose.

    d. Look for a possible consultant in the psychiatric nursing department, school of nursing, department of psychiatry, or your own unit.

4. Have one or more planning meetings to decide the following:
    a. Purpose for the group.
    b. How often to meet.
    c. How long to meet (e.g., 45 minutes, bimonthly).
    d. Who should lead the group.
    e. How to know it is working and how to know it is not working.

REFERENCES

Bilodeau, C. The nurse and her reactions to critical care nursing. *Heart and Lung*, 1973, 2, 358-363.

Cassem, N., & Hackett, T. Stress on the nurse and therapist in the intensive care unit and the coronary care unit. *Heart and Lung*, 1975, 4, 252-259.

Cooper, S. Mental health consultation workshop, Ann Arbor, Mich., June 14-16, 1976.

Davis, A. Ethics rounds with intensive care nurses. *Nursing Clinics of North America*, 1979, 14(1), 45-55.

Deloughery, G., Neuman, B., & Gebbie, K. Change in problem-solving ability among nurses receiving mental health consultation: A pilot study. *Communicating Nursing Research, 3*, Denver: WICHE, 1970.

Di Mars, J. Personal communication, Winter, 1979.

Garrant, C. The psychiatric liaison nurse—an interpretation of the role. *Supervisor Nurse*, 1977, 8, 75-78.

Hay, D., & Oken, D. The psychological stress of intensive care unit nursing. *Psychosomatic Medicine*, 1972, 34, 109-118.

Holsclaw, P. Nursing in high emotional risk areas. *Nursing Forum*, 1965, 4(4), 37-45.

Johnson, B. Psychiatric nurse consultant in a general hospital. *Nursing Outlook*, 1963, 11, 728-729.

Jones, E. Who supports the nurse? *Nursing Outlook*, 1962, 10, 476-478.

Kolson, G. Mental health nursing consultation: A study of expectations. *Journal of Psychiatric Nursing and Mental Health Services*, August 1976, 13, 24-32.

Kornfeld, D. S. Psychiatric problems of an intensive care unit. *Medical Clinics of North America*, 1971, 55, 1353-1363.

Koumans, A. J. R. Psychiatric consultation in an intensive care unit. *JAMA*, 1965, 194, 163-167.

Mannino, F. Effecting change through consultation. In F. Mannino, B. MacLennan, & M. Shore (Eds.). *The practice of mental health consultation*. New York: Halsted Press, 1975.

Nelson, J., & Schilke, D. The evolution of psychiatric liaison nursing. *Perspectives in Psychiatric Care*, 1976, 14(2), 60-65.

Przepiorka, K., & Bender, L. Psychiatric nursing consultation in a university medical center. *Hospital and Community Psychiatry*, 1977, 28, 755-758,

Roberts, S. *Behavioral concepts and the critically ill patient*. Englewood Cliffs, N.J.: Prentice-Hall, 1976.

Robinson, L. *Liaison nursing: Psychological approach to patient care*. Philadelphia: F. A. Davis, 1974.

Shubin, S. RX for stress—Your stress. *Nursing 79*, 1979, 9(1), 53-55.

Simon, N., & Whiteley, S. Psychiatric consultation with MICU nurses: The consultation conference as a working group. *Heart and Lung*, 1977, 6, 497-504.

Youngner, S., Jackson, D., & Allen, M. Staff attitudes towards the care of the critically ill in the medical intensive care unit. *Critical Care Medicine*, 1979, 7(2), 35-40.

CHAPTER 11

Regulating stress through physical activity

Patty Zindler-Wernet

My purpose . . . . is to expand the awareness of the limits of the body and its capacity for change—to communicate the body is change.

Don Johnson

A PERSONAL PERSPECTIVE

My interest in stress began when I worked as a nurse practioner in a clinic with children who had genetic, chronic, and terminal illnesses. As a part of continuity of care, I visited my patients while they were hospitalized, and on a number of occasions, I was on the unit when a child was confronted with a painful procedure or died. Two incidents were particularly distressing to me. I remember a 10-year-old boy with leukemia who, when told that a second bone marrow transplant operation was required, became hysterical and cried, "I want to die!" I also remember two 8-year-old friends in the hematology clinic who had been admitted in critical condition to the hospital at the same time. When one died, her friend asked me why the nurses were so quiet and sad. I was not able to tell her because I had been instructed by the physician to say nothing. He, like many of the physicians with whom I worked, had difficulty dealing with the death of young children and, particularly, talking to their families about it. As a consequence, this burden fell on me or the social worker. It only added to my worry and concern at succeeding in my new extended role as a nurse practitioner.

Because other nurses in the clinic seemed to resent my graduate preparation and assessment skills, working relationships often became strained, especially when my role was questioned. I came to doubt my own feelings of productivity and well-being. In addition, the pressures of too little time to do the things that had to be done and the crowded environment of the small trailer in which I worked became increasingly stressful. I had trouble getting out of bed in the morning. The muscles in

101

my neck and shoulders ached, and my body felt stiff. My energy level was at an all-time low. Although I was only 26 years old, I felt much, much older. After 6 months of muscle spasms, stiffness, and profound changes in my self-image, I decided that something had to be done.

MANIFESTATIONS OF JOB-RELATED STRESS

What I have related about job-induced stress is not unique in nursing or in many of the jobs that deal with high levels of stress. Many of the psychosocial demands that I experienced have been expressed by nurses in other settings. Conflicts with physicians, co-workers, and supervisors; the pressure of getting tasks done in a limited amount of time; and dealing with death and dying reflect environmental demands to which nurses respond, irrespective of the setting in which they work. There also are other job factors, such as standing for long hours in one position, the noise of complex machines, and other sensory stimuli that impact on the minds and bodies of nurses.

Since many nurses work under heavy environmental demands, as described in Chapter 6, they often experience chronic tension and fatigue. For some nurses this stress becomes suppressed pain, which is no longer obvious even to them. Yet, the energy that is necessary to dull this pain could better be used to work with patients and their families. It has been suggested that chronic energy loss, when added to the energy required simply to get the job done every day, can have a causal relationship to illness. Complaints such as insomnia, headaches, inability to concentrate, fatigue, upset stomach, and other symptoms may, indeed, signal stress overload and lead to other manifestations of disease (Pelletier, 1977). If nurses experience problems that disrupt their own well-being, they cannot be expected to attend to the well-being of their patients.

It is possible, however, to break the pattern of stress before chronic illness results. What is required is a willingness to listen to the body and understand its symptoms. Nurses have been trained to assess the patient and observe body changes. It is equally important that they be sensitive to their own body signals and take responsibility for caring for themselves.

ROLE OF PHYSICAL ACTIVITY IN REDUCING STRESS
Physiological studies

Although there are conflicting views about the value of physical activity as a means of dealing with stress, there is increasing evidence that it has positive physical and mental effects (Kostrubala, 1977).

Physical activities have been classified as aerobic or nonaerobic, depending on whether they result in accelerated heart rate. The importance of aerobic exercises such as jogging, walking, skiing, swimming, and biking is that they improve the cardiovascular system, as evidence by lower pulse rate, lower blood pressure, and increased peripheral blood flow (Eliot, Forker, & Robinson, 1976). These changes may be the most critical factors in reducing stress. Aerobic exercise also requires greater oxygen consumption because of sustained physical exertion. This, in turn, stimulates the enzyme system and results in increased blood flow. There are also beneficial effects in the respiratory and muscular systems (Ardell, 1979).

Mental health and physical activity

One of the most important benefits of physical activity is the sense of well-being that it elicits, in addition to providing a focus for a sense of personal control, both in terms of oneself and the stressful environment (Gal & Lazarus, 1975). This sense of mastery and the resulting reduction of anxiety still can remain, even if the activity does not provide complete control over the situation. Aerobic exercise has recently been regarded as one treatment plan for depression (Greist, Klein, Eischens, Faris, Gurman, & Morgan, 1979). In one study (Solomon & Bumpus, 1978) running was seen to offer sustained improvements in measurable changes of depression levels when compared before and after a 6- to 10-week program.

Is running of value in the alleviation of depression only because of some "time-out factor," in getting away from stressful situations, or are there actual physical changes in the body? There are currently two answers to this question. One explanation is that exercise may burn up energy that otherwise might sustain feelings of anxiety. Other researchers (Kostrubala, 1977) insist that running is therapeutic not just because of its expenditure of energy. In one study (Higdon, 1978) running in single doses worked better than tranquilizers as a relaxant for symptoms of anxiety tension, and without undesired side effects.

Although it is not certain exactly how the benefits of physical activity relieve stress, researchers agree that it does promote physical and mental changes.

PHYSICAL ACTIVITY MODALITIES

In a profession in which nurses are educated to be constantly alert to the body changes of patients, it is important that nurses learn more about their own bodies. Because it may be difficult to find ways to relieve stress at work, it seems obligatory for nurses to build their "physical and emotional muscle" away from the job. Nurses, especially, may feel that after a hectic day at work, there simply is not enough reserve energy to engage in additional physical activities. However, the energy expended at work cannot be a substitute for the positive energy derived from physical activities (Dychtwald, 1977). Some of the most basic exercise modalities include yoga (with breathing and centering qualities), body therapies (Feldenkrais, Rolfing), and aerobic exercise (running).

Yoga

Yoga is one of the oldest forms of exercise. It also can be a useful preparation in readying the body for aerobic exercise such as running. Yoga stretches the muscles to balance the body's energy and thus relieves tension. Movements are performed in a relaxed, slow motion, with few repetitions. These sessions, according to Jackson (1979), leave one feeling elevated and revitalized. Yoga encourages the use of separate body parts for more flexibility. If one's neck or spine is stiff, looking to the side or looking backward can be difficult, and as a result, one's perception of the world can become narrowed. The consequences of self-narrowed physical perceptions may limit one's appraisal and perceptions of stressors, personal body manifestations, and ways of filtering them.

Body therapies

Physical activities that redefine body awareness involve the reestablishment of communication between the brain and parts of the body that may no longer respond to voluntary control. Under stress, for instance, a person may respond with exaggerated patterns of body movements. This may include holding the breath and tensing the muscles, which increases anxiety and a general inability to function. When the kinesthetic sense is distorted, the awareness of the body deteriorates (Masters & Houston, 1978).

One way to change these patterns is to give the person repeated experiences so that the nervous system will decide that good use is preferable. Faulty patterns can then be sensed so that the body can begin to correct itself.

Feldenkrais. Feldenkrais is one method of developing body and mind awareness through various exercises that can be done by oneself. It was developed by Moshe Feldenkrais, who believed that by working with the neuromuscular connections of both the body and the mind, one's body awareness and self-image could be improved (Feldenkrais, 1972). Feldenkrais has designed thousands of movement exercises based on how people use their body in repetitive patterns. These patterns, however, are often limiting and restrictive. Although they serve a function, they keep individuals from making fuller use of their bodies. Feldenkrais exercises encourage people to become more aware of themselves and their potential. They are often so unusual in form and practice that they force people to explore and integrate aspects of themselves of which they probably have been unaware.

In a group class, for instance, a therapist may direct exercises for the left shoulder. The shoulder becomes increasingly free, and the group's attention is focused on the sensation of the movement. By imagining the movements and sensations for the right shoulder, the comparison becomes instructive to the conscious mind. These same exercises can then be used for the right shoulder as the body learns to transfer the kinesthetic imagery from one side of the body to the other.

Feldenkrais exercises can be helpful in enhancing many physical activities. In running, large muscles are used, whereas in Feldenkrais exercises, smaller muscle groups are used. Feldenkrais can assist one in learning about subtle changes in the body, which can increase body awareness with fewer resulting physical injuries.

Rolfing. Rolfing is a system of "deep muscular manipulation and massage," developed by Dr. Ida Rolf, a biochemist and physiologist. Key concepts in the Rolfing method include the following. The body is not thought to be a fixed unit but one that can be anatomically ordered and realigned into different postural placements. A body out of alignment is especially susceptible to gravity. Slumping positions, for example, are impossible to correct simply by standing straight because the connective tissues already have been set in place. This, in turn, causes other parts of the body to compensate and so creates further imbalance (Johnson, 1977).

In the Rolfing method the connective tissues are realigned by pressure applied by the therapist's hands, fingers, knuckles, and elbows sliding over the skin. There are ten sessions, the first seven of which concentrate primarily on individual parts of the body, such as the chest, legs, pelvis, and head. The last three sessions reintegrate the whole body along its new line.

During a Rolfing session, I became aware that under times of tension I would hold my breath. Tensing my muscles would bring about pain, but breathing, rather than holding my breath, brought about the release of tension. In these sessions I also recognized that my learned stance included holding my chin out and up. When I was made aware of this and corrected it, I felt more at ease and there was less strain in my neck and shoulders. Coincidentally, a group of nurses with whom I worked asked me why I no longer appeared to be so arrogant, which they had equated with my jutting chin. The relief of my tension and pain had allowed by body to assume a more stress-free posture and develop a heightened vitality and awareness.

Running

Benefits. According to Daws (1977), the failure to evoke political and social change in the 1960s has resulted in the internalization of those efforts. There is an emphasis on going back inside one's body for a sense of accomplishment and fitness. Exercise physiologists content that running is the most beneficial and efficient of the various aerobic exercises. Cooper (1977) developed a point system to measure the value of running and other aerobic exercises based on the level of oxygen used to perform them. The amount was standardized, and a point value was assigned to each exercise so that a training schedule could be devised on the basis of age and ability. For instance, by maintaining the heart rate to approximately 75% of its work load for at least 12 minutes a day, four times a week, the heart can be conditioned sufficiently to withstand the daily stresses demanded of the cardiovascular system.

Running, like any physical fitness program, must be done on a regular and consistent basis if its benefits are to be realized. Although running four to seven times a week requires commitment, it can be fun. Running can also be a social outlet and a way to meet new people. It provides an opportunity to choose a variety of environmental settings and to select those which hold special interest. It is also an activity that requires a minimum of equipment and expense.

The importance of running to me is not technique or training, or what shoes to wear, or what to eat, or what exercises to do, but rather, knowing what is possible for my body to accomplish and then surpassing the initial image I had of myself. Running is not only a body experience; it is an exercising of the mind as well. Exhilaration or euphoria occurs in running sustained distances. Sensory images change as well: The quality of color, hues, and intensities of one's surroundings become more vivid. Problems that may have seemed ambiguous and overwhelming become more definite and resolved after a 30- to 40-minute run (Kostrubala, 1977). At this point, running became, for me, what Glasser (1976) calls a "positive addiction." I was excited to discover that much of what I had read about running actually was true. I *did* feel a greater sense of physical well-being and personal control. Not only did I notice changes that could be measured by blood pressure, pulse, and weight but there was a sense of mastery and self-confidence.

Running program for nurses. To provide an opportunity to experience the benefits of running, a jogging club at Stanford University Hospital was begun with a group of nurses. Goals were defined, the first of which was to "walk-run" a mile in 12 minutes. This was followed by a series of 1-hour lecture/discussion groups about proper clothing and shoes, calculating the individual's heart training rate, and warm-up and postrunning exercises.

The sessions started with stretching exercises. A mile course was plotted, and all the nurses ran together, no matter what their ability or how long it took them. It seemed important to the nurses that I run with them, since I was a nurse and director of the running program. After the experience in running, we spent time talking about the effects of running, such as body sensations, changes in moods, and other effects.

At the end of this 10-week running program, several nurses made commitments to run with each other. All had improved by running faster or by increasing their distance.

Guidelines for running. The following guidelines, which were developed to assist in the running program, were helpful:

1. Make a commitment to yourself that you will run for at least 6 weeks before quitting.
2. Run at least 4 days a week. Start with 12 minutes each session, and work up to 30 minutes.
3. Run with another person or a group, since it will assist you in making a commitment to yourself and to the group to run.
4. If you are a woman, run with other women or run with people who run at your pace.
5. Run only as fast as you can while still talking to a running partner.
6. Set a reasonable goal, such as running 3 miles by the end of 6 months.
7. If you become injured or overstressed, take a few days off until the problem seems resolved.
8. If you are bored, select a new place to run.
9. Join a jogging club for inspiration and new friends.
10. Keep a record of your fitness index.

Sheehan (1978) offered the following suggestions for measuring fitness: When awaking in the morning, lie in bed for 5 minutes and then take your pulse and record your weight. Take your pulse immediately after running and then 15 minutes later; record these figures over the week. You will see a weekly improvement until a lower resting heart rate is attained, usually around 60 beats per minute. Be aware of any sudden rise. If the morning pulse is up 10 beats or more, you have not recovered from your previous day's training. Practice therefore should be eliminated or curtailed until the pulse returns to normal.

Profile of nurses who run. Fifteen nurses (6 from the Stanford running program) who had been running from about 6 months to 6 years were interviewed. Their age range was 24 to 47 years. One half of the nurses were married, worked 20 to 40 hours a week on a hospital unit, and ran from 2 to 6 miles a day. The following questions were asked:

1. What inspired you to start running?
2. Do you think nurses have more difficulties in starting to run than other professionals?
3. How do you manage to combine running with your life-style?
4. Free response.

Responses to question 1 indicated that approximately one half of the nurses started running to lose weight, whereas the other half observed a friend or mate running and were impressed by the benefits. Nurses were unanimous in their belief that they did not perceive it was more difficult for them to get started in a running program than for members of other professions. They noted, however, that the mental strains of patient care, inherent in their nursing role, did make it difficult at times to continue the program. The majority of nurses responded to question 3 by stating that the best time to run was immediately after their workday before going home (except the evening shift, who ran before work).

Many of the nurses commented on the simplicity of the activity and the "mental highs." One nurse stated, "The more hectic the day, the more I wanted to run at the end of the shift." Some nurses noted that their running program depended more on what was happening at home than at work. Married nurses with children felt that their husbands' support was vital, and those who had small children indicated that it was the only time when they could be alone. Several nurses described running as an "inexpensive psychiatrist," whereas others perceived running as taking responsibility for their own well-being. Most felt that they had accomplished a goal which had seemed impossible before.

Perhaps, one nurse said it best of all, "Everyone wins in running."

SUMMARY

The development of my own body awareness to relieve stress did not happen at work. My initial resistance to physical activity went back to experiences of early physical education with failed activities, such as missing a volleyball in an important game, fragmented instruction, and inadequate facilities for women. It is difficult to believe that 10 years ago women were not allowed to run over 6 miles in official competitions. The belief was that women could not take the strenuous activity or the pressure (Tutko, 1978). For many years women were socialized against the same strenuous physical activities for stress reduction that men had practiced for years. When a woman can say, "I am capable, I can do it," then she is more likely to look at external pressures and stress and decide on ways of managing them.

Nurses have learned to work competently under stress at the price of tensions, fatigue, and even unconsciously suppressed pain levels. The energy nurses put into ineffectively dulling this stress and pain is to hide the obvious from themselves and their patients. Nurses lose energy that they need in working with their patients and families and in pursuing new ideas and new ways of looking at their environment. Nurses can become energy "zappers" for the very people they are trying to assist, instead of professionals who promote healing. The manifestations of stress (i.e., colds, muscle tension, headaches, high blood pressure, poor appetite, insomnia, and so on) are a message from within the body.

My own orientation in dealing with stress has been mainly with physical activity. There are endless paths to body awareness and regulating stress, of which the ones in this chapter are only a few. Whichever paths are taken, the responsibility for self-care resides in each person. Interactions with other people can then become loving, caring, and more perceptive, which to me is the essence of nursing.

REFERENCES

Ardell, D. *High level wellness*. New York: Bantam Books, 1979.

Cooper, K. *The aerobics way*. New York: Bantam Books, 1977.

Daws, R. *The self-made Olympian*. Mountain View, Calif.: World Publications, 1977.

Dychtwald, K. *Bodymind*. New York: Pantheon Books, 1977.

Eliot, R. S., Forker, A. D., & Robertson, R. J. Aerobic exercise as a therapeutic modality in the relief of stress. *Advances in Cardiology*, 1976, *18*, 231-242.

Feldenkrais, M. *Awareness through movement*. New York: Harper & Row, 1972.

Gal, R., & Lazarus, R. The role of activity in anticipating and confronting stressful situations. *Journal of Human Stress*, 1975, *1*(4), 4-20.

Glasser, W. *Positive addiction*. New York: Harper & Row, 1976.

Greist, J., Klein, M., Eischens, R., Faris, J.,

Gurman, A., & Morgan, W. Running as treatment for depression. *Comprehensive Psychiatry*, 1979, 20(1), 41-54.

Higdon, J. Can running cure mental illness? *Runner's World*, January 1978, 36-43.

Jackson, I. Yoga for the runner. In *Runner's World, New Exercise for Runners*. Mountain View, Calif.: World Publications, 1979.

Johnson, D. *The protean body*. New York: Harper & Row, 1977.

Kostrubala, T. *The joy of running*. New York: Pocket Books, 1977.

Masters, R., & Houston, J. *Listening to the body*. New York: Delacorte Press, 1978.

Pelletier, K. *Mind as healer: Mind as slayer*. New York: Delacorte, 1977.

Sheehan, G. *Running and being: The total experience*. New York: Warner Books, 1978.

Solomon, E. G., & Bumpus, A. K. The running meditation response: An adjunct to psychotherapy. *American Journal of Psychotherapy*, 1978, *32*, 583-592.

Tutko, T. The psychology of competition. In *The complete woman runner*. Mountain View, Calif.: World Publications, 1978.

SUGGESTED READINGS

Benson, J. *Relaxation response*. New York: Avon Books, 1975.

Downing, G. *The massage book*. New York: Random House, 1972.

Ferguson, T. Exercise in self care. *Medical Self-Care: Access to Medical Tools*, 1978, *3*, 8-23.

Fixx, J. *The complete book of running*. New York: Random House, 1977.

Glover, B., & Shepherd, J. *The runner's handbook*. New York: Penguin Books, 1978.

Gunter, B. *Sense relaxation—Below your mind*. New York: Collier Books, 1978.

Kurtz R., & Prestera, H. *The body reveals: An illustrated guide to the psychology of the body*. New York: Harper & Row, 1976.

Leonard, G. *The ultimate athlete*. New York: Viking Press, 1975.

Lilliefors, J. *Total running*. New York: W. Morrow, 1979.

Murphy, M., & White, K. *The psychic side of sports*. Reading, Mass.: Addison-Wesley, 1978.

Porter, D. *Inner running*. New York: Ace Books, 1978.

Rowen, L., & Winkler, B. *The working woman's body book*. New York: Rawson, 1978.

Rush, A. K. *Getting clear: Bodywork for women*. New York: Random House, 1973.

Schafer, W. *Stress, distress and growth*. Davis, Calif.: Dialogue Books, 1978.

Spino, M. *Beyond jogging: The interspaces of running*. Millbrae, Calif.: Celestial Arts, 1976.

Thie, J. *Touch for health*. Marina Del Rey, Calif.: De Vorss, 1973.

Ulloyt, J. *Women running*. Mountain View, Calif.: World Publications, 1976.

CHAPTER 12

From distress and worry to awareness and fulfillment: perspectives of a critical care nurse

Judith Ann Moran

A DAY OF REMEMBRANCE AND RESOLUTION

My resolve to care for critically ill patients began a number of years ago when I was a student nurse in a large medical center in upstate New York.

I vividly recall being with my patient, Mr. E, a 55-year-old man who was recovering from a myocardial infarction. Mr. E was preparing to return home in a few days, and we were discussing travel—and then it happened. He suddenly slumped into a chair. I shook him . . . no response. I frantically called for help. Before I knew it, I was suddenly being shoved aside by two registered nurses and two physicians. I can still see the grim, stressful looks on their faces as they asked: "What happened to him?" Although in a state of shock and disbelief, I managed to mumble, "I don't know. He just collapsed." I could feel the tension as the names of life-saving drugs and equipment were briskly ordered. Nurses quickly responded and snatched drugs and equipment from the "crash" cart. Everyone seemed to know exactly what to do—everyone, that is, but me. The tempo increased. "What is the rhythm? Ventricular fibrillation. Let's defibrillate. . . Hurry up? No response. . . .again, defibrillate." The physician who seemed to be doing most of the procedures called for a pacing wire and inserted it transvenously. As the nurse connected it to the pacemaker, the rhythm now was agonal. "How long have we been at it?" "Thirty minutes," was the reply. The chief resident looked defeated. "Pupils are fixed and dilated. No blood pressure. I think that is it. We have done all we can do. He had very severe heart disease." Then the final order followed, "Someone be sure to notify the attending physician, and don't forget to remind him to call the family." I could not help but wonder if the physician would remember to tell the family, and how could he possibly begin to tell them that their loved one had died.

From utter chaos the atmosphere changed to chilling silence. I recall my feelings of disbelief, shock, and grief. I said to myself, "It can't be over; he can't be dead. You all can't leave." I had never seen anyone die before. Many, many thoughts flashed through my mind. "He had just been talking to me. Maybe I should have done something? But what? What had happened?" I later learned that Mr. E had died from a massive pulmonary embolus. I wanted to know why. He was such a nice man, and he was doing so well. The vital signs that I had taken were fine. He did not complain of any pain. "Could I have helped in some way?" I worried for weeks about my ineptitude and the fate of Mr. E. My worry was replaced by my resolution to continue my education and become a critical care nurse.

AN AFTERTHOUGHT

Since that day, in 1970, I have had many similar experiences in my role as a master's-prepared critical care nurse. In my expanded role the question are always many, and the answers far too few and indefinite. The experience of traumatic and sudden death is still difficult for me to cope with. Even though I now know exactly how to function in these emergency situations, the events of death continue to elicit stressful feelings and responses. Somehow I am sustained by new knowledge, by continuous growth and understanding, and by feelings within me that I can adapt in positive, productive ways.

MY ROLE AS A CRITICAL CARE NURSE

It has been a decade since I resolved to care for critically ill patients. I find my role challenging and rewarding. I enjoy the nature of work that includes aspects of both autonomy and effective teamwork. The tasks are varied and numerous, for example, (1) assisting with and doing physical assessments; (2) contributing to the establishment of a diagnosis; (3) continuously problem solving and decision making; (4) following physician's directions; and most of all, (5) giving total care through meeting the needs of helpless patients.

The role of the critical care nurse can be so exciting that you forget how exhausting and demanding the hectic pace of the acute care setting can be. You forget until you almost fall asleep while driving home from the night shift. You could cry because you are so physically exhausted. All you can think about is sleep. However, once safely in bed, all you can think about is: "Did I finish that chart? Did I chart that medication? Did

I remind the other nurse of the patient's drug allergies, of his fear of being alone, of his past medical history? I need to remind the head nurse that the suture sets are worthless. The next time I see Dr. Jones we will have to discuss his attitude with some of the patients."

A constant vacillation of emotions and thoughts occurs in the minds of those who work in the critical care setting. A factor contributing to this thought process, and one of the major sources of stress, is the continuous variation in pace inherent in these environments. One hour can be slow and quiet. Suddenly, emergencies arise, and there is an overwhelming bombardment of needs and demands. The anxiety, tension, and stress can rise until it is seemingly unbearable. You want it all to stop for a moment so that you can think clearly. You only have two hands; it can't all be done right this minute, but it has to! Hurry up . . . hurry up!! Sound familiar? Can you feel your blood pressure rising just remembering situations like that?

MY PERSPECTIVES IN DEVELOPING AWARENESS AND MANAGING STRESS

Critical care nurses feel the full physiological and psychological effects of the stress response to demands in the ICU environment. However, some nurses—those who elect to continue to work in the ICU—manage to adapt to the highly variable, but ever-present stresses. Some nurses appear to manage the stress more effectively than others. They learn to (1) use the energy from the stress response in constructive, positive ways; (2) withstand the physically demanding requirements of admitting major medical, trauma, or postoperative surgical cases; (3) cope with the frustration of confused, anoxic, critically ill patients; and (4) repeat monotonous procedures, such as peritoneal dialysis, over and over again.

To manage stress effectively and to achieve the necessary "filtering," it seems essential that the ICU nurse be able to recognize and understand four major components of the stress concept, as presented in Chapter 2: (1) the stimuli and demands inherent in the ICU environment; (2) the nurse's own unique appraisal and perception of the ICU; (3) the dynamics of the psychological, physiological, and sociological responses to the ICU stressors; and (4) the manner of responding and adapting to these environmental factors.

I have found that it is helpful, in learning to manage stress effectively, to begin by assessing the way I characteristically respond to everyday pressures and demands. Asking myself the following questions seems helpful: "What situations make me feel uncomfortable? Why? How do I feel during these times? How do I look during these times? For example, does uncertainty make me feel uneasy, uptight, hot, tense, flushed, or shaky?"

Once the process of exploring, appraising, and assessing how one responds to the environmental demands of the ICU is accomplished, one may be able to adapt in more positive ways. Nurses can use the process to filter the demands and thereby nullify the harmful effects of stress. For example, in an ICU situation, where numerous demands are being placed on nurses for their time, attention, and expertise, stress responses are often triggered. It may be difficult to set priorities or to get anything done under such circumstances. However, there are things that can be done to cope with these experiences. When nurses sense stress mounting within them and disorganization about to result, they can pause momentarily, take a few deep breaths, and tell themselves to relax and that things will get done . . . one thing at a time . . . first things first.

In situations where such intrapersonal positive feedback is impossible, and all attempts to filter the stressors fail, options are still available for effective stress management by nurses. They can express their feelings to a co-worker in an attempt to gain strength and support. All too frequently, people believe that expressing fears and anxieties may be viewed as a sign of professional weakness (unprofessional behavior). Such a perception only facilitates maladaptive responses and adds heightened conflict to the environment.

Another technique that nurses can use to reduce feelings of stress is to focus on patient teaching. This will probably not only calm and reduce the stress experienced by the patient but will benefit the nurse as a result of the patient's positive responses.

Professional nurses share the common goal of wanting to prevent and ease suffering. They are frequently confronted by the dilemma of having to assist with, or to perform, treatments that are necessary but unpleasant and sometimes painful, such as starting IVs, changing dressings on wounds, endotracheal suctioning, and many other procedures. Discussing one's feelings, engendered by these procedures, can (1) assist the nurse to identify the demanding tasks in these situations, (2) identify ways in which these demands can be reduced, and (3) identify methods to increase efficacy of adaptive mechanisms through verbalizing and filtering the stressful impact of these procedures and situations.

Patients, as well as nurses, respond in unique ways to experiences that they encounter in the ICU environment. It can be perplexing for the nurse to understand, for example, why one patient reacts violently when suctioned, whereas another does not seem to be threatened by it. At the same time some nurses dislike suctioning patients, while other nurses are not bothered by doing the procedure. It takes experience, built on continuous questioning and learning, to understand the dynamics of the idiosyncrasies of individual responses and perceptions. A mutual sharing of thought, insights, and knowledge may also enhance the ability of ICU nurses to anticipate and adapt to the vast variety of stimuli that surround them.

Because I have learned so much through experiences with my patients, colleagues, the Stress Management Program, and my doctoral studies, I would like to put it all together and present my story about Betty and how I cared for her.

A CASE STUDY
An ICU nurse and her patient

It was in late September when Betty was struck by a car on her way home from school. On arrival in the Emergency Room, she was in severe shock. Stabilization was difficult because of major blood loss; multiple organ, tissue, and skeletal injuries; and severe cerebral trauma. Physicians from neurosurgery, general surgery, orthopedics, thoracic surgery, urology, and plastic surgery worked with Betty for 8 hours in the operating room.

I was working in the surgical ICU on the morning that Betty was admitted from the OR. She was the epitome of a major trauma case. I remember thinking how severely injured she looked. She appeared so small and fragile under the mass of traction and dressings. Her face was grotesquely distorted by the edema, secondary to her facial and skull injuries. The craniotomy dressing seemed enormous. Her eyes were swollen shut, making it extremely difficult to check her pupils. They were reactive but slightly irregular in size. Spastic, jerky movements were visible on the left side of her body, but the right side remained totally flaccid. A tracheostomy tube was attached to an MA-I ventilator. Her shallow, erratic respirations made it imperative that mechanical ventilation be used to control her breathing. Two chest tubes exited from her left chest and were attached to Pleur-evac. A large abdominal dressing covered the laparotomy incision. A nasogastric tube was connected to intermittent suction. The returns were blood tinged. A central venous pressure line had been inserted into the right subclavian vein, and two peripheral IVs were also inserted to infuse electrolyte solutions and blood. She appeared pale, and her skin was cold and clammy. Her hematocrit was 27% (normal value = 37 to 47 ml/100 ml). Vital signs on admission were as follows: blood pressure, 80/50 mm Hg; pulse rate 120 beats per minute (sinus tachycardia); central venous pressure, 3 mm Hg; temperature, 36.5° C.

Betty's admission from the OR to the ICU was hectic. Vital signs needed to be taken every 15 minutes because they were unstable. Her physical assessment was an extremely complicated process. There were numerous IVs to be regulated, tubes to be connected, types of drainage to measure, and IV fluid replacements to calculate. Physicians from many services surrounded her bed. Each physician gave orders on what he wanted done immediately . . . many of which overlapped, conflicted, or both. "I told you to do this now; don't bother doing that!" I could feel my heartbeat racing and my blood pressure rising. I wanted to yell, "STOP! QUIET! EVERYONE GO AWAY . . . LET ME THINK . . . LET ME GET ORGANIZED!!" But no, the questions and orders kept coming . . . "What is the blood pressure now? I told you to change that dressing a few minutes ago—isn't it done yet? That IV is almost out. Hurry up. Come on. Let's get some more blood going . . . HURRY!!!!!"

My next major area of concern was Betty's family. I knew that they had been waiting for many long hours. I wondered if any of the physicians had spoken with them. I realized that things in the unit were not going to quiet down for some time, and I was able to have another nurse take over for me while I went to meet the family. As I walked closer to the waiting room, I could hear voices saying, "Something must be wrong. It's taking so long. Maybe they forgot us?"

Dialogue

Nurse (J. M.): Hello. Mrs. L? My name is J. M. I am the nurse who has been taking care of Betty. Another nurse is with her right now. Have the doctors spoken with you?

Mrs. L: Yes, the doctors . . . I forget their names. They told me that it wasn't good. Is that true? What's the matter?

Nurse (J. M.): She was very badly hurt. Right now her vital signs are a little unstable. But we are watching her very carefully, every second of the time. We are all doing everything we possibly can to help her.

Mrs. L: Can we see her now? This is my mother, father, and Betty's sister, Mary.

Nurse (J. M.): Yes, you can see her now, two of you at a time because the room that she is in is small. Also, for now I'll ask you to stay just a few minutes because things are so busy. You can come back a little later on. I'll let you know when. We won't forget you. Now, I want to tell you a few things. I want you all to know what to expect when you see Betty. First of all, the room is filled with equipment. Most of it is surrounding Betty's bed. A lot of it makes strange noises, but that is normal. Just that can be upsetting if you haven't seen it before. There are also lots of nurses and doctors around her. It will be very busy in there.

Betty has a large bandage on her head. There is a little blood on it too, but that is O.K. Her face is swollen and black and blue. The swelling will go down and it will look better soon. Her right arm and leg are broken, so the doctors put them in traction. They look like they are hanging from ropes that are tied to bars over her bed. (I elevated my arm to try to show them how it would look.) She has a breathing tube in her neck, a tracheostomy tube. A machine is attached to it that is helping her breathe. It's called a ventilator, or respirator. It gives her the oxygen that she needs, and it lets her rest. She won't be able to open her eyes or respond to you. But she may be able to hear you if you speak to her. Do you have any questions?

Mrs. L: So much has happened. I don't know. It seems like she just went to school and now . . . I don't know.

Nurse (J. M.): I know that it's hard to understand all of this now. You need time to sort it all out. But I know from other families who have gone through this same type of experience that it helps to know what to expect when you see Betty for the first time. She'll look very different to you. She will look very hurt, but that is because of the serious accident. I only wish that I could say more to help you. Are you ready to go see her now?

Mrs. L: Thank you. I think that it did help me. Can my father and I go in first?

Nurse (J. M.): That will be fine. Let's just go to the door and I'll see if everything is O.K. so we can go in.

Mrs. L: Dad, come with me. Then Mom and Mary can go in to see Betty.

I stayed close to Mrs. L as we entered the room. For the first time I saw Betty not as a patient but as a person—as Mrs. L's little girl. Before this moment she had been another trauma patient. The experience of personalization, of humanization, had occurred on re-entering the room. Mrs. L walked closer to the bed. Her father followed her. He did not look at Betty but only at his own daughter. Mrs. L reached down and touched her child's hand.

Mrs. L: It's O.K., honey . . . Mommy's here. It's all right.

(She only looked at her child's face). After a few minutes she turned, and taking her father's hand, they left the room. Looking straight ahead . . . pale, silent, expressionless . . . she seemed dazed.

At this point the other nurse had several questions that had to be answered immediately. Therefore I was unable to walk Mrs. L and her father back into the waiting room. I hoped that they had made it. I felt sad that I couldn't be with them to give them the support they needed. Before I knew it, Mary and Betty's grandmother were entering the room. They appeared horrified by the sight before them. Mary was crying; her grandmother was motionless. They started to back out of the room. I was able to help them back to the waiting room.

Nurse (J. M.): This has been a very difficult experience for all of you. I hope that it helps you to know that Betty doesn't feel any pain. She doesn't know what's happening. We are doing everything that we can for Betty.

It seemed so little to say. I felt frustrated and helpless. I had to go back into Betty's room now. I promised the family that I would not forget them. I had to go. What if Betty were my sister? What if I were Betty? Why do these things happen? These were the thoughts running through my mind as I walked back to the ICU.

Betty's room looked like a disaster area. The initial chaos had subsided, but I wondered when it would all start up again. Most of the physicians had left the unit, leaving a multitude of orders.

I pondered where to start as I looked at Betty. Somehow she looked so peaceful. Had her vital signs stabilized? Was I just getting used to looking at her . . . or was it because I now saw her as a person, instead of just as a patient with a lot of problems? The mass of IVs and equipment seemed incidental. Was I feeling more relaxed because now the hectic pace, the uncertainty, the ambiguity of her case were more under control? I knew what had been done and what still needed to be done. I knew the extent of her injuries and what had transpired in the OR. I had time to do a thorough physical assessment. I felt, for the first time, as though I knew what was going on and could organize and plan Betty's case. Before the physicians had left the unit, I had been able to ask many pertinent questions about Betty's condition. I knew what to look for and what to expect in her vital signs and responses. I was cognizant of the numerous alterations and complications that might occur at any moment, fully realizing the unpredictable nature of multiple trauma cases. I knew my role as a critical care nurse and what I had to do to give the care she needed to survive.

COMA AND CAREGIVING OVER TIME

Although Betty's vital signs had remained stable during the 3 months that she was in the ICU, and nothing was actually wrong, nothing seemed right either. Betty had never regained consciousness. Optimism and hope were starting to run a little thin for the family, as well as for the nurses, as the Christmas holiday season drew near. Betty's physicians could offer no explanation for her sustained state of coma. All of the cerebral arteriograms and other tests looked normal. Their comments ranged from, "It takes time" or "I just don't know" to a shrug of the shoulders.

My faith was also becoming strained. However, when the family came to visit, I managed to support them and say, "Everything is stable. There don't seem to be any changes, but we have hope." The family clung to every word. They evaluated every facial expression for some sign, some small indication of improvement, to sustain their own hope.

I continued to work closely with Betty thoughout the long weeks of her stay in the ICU. I encouraged Betty's family to bring in some of her favorite things—a stuffed animal, pictures of her with her family and friends, and a doll from her younger years. Another nurse (S. L.) and I would relate to these things in our daily conversations with Betty. We would also play music on the radio. Betty's room was active, cheerful, and bright. I distinctly remember positioning Betty's bed so that when the curtains were open, the sun would shine on her. The warmth of the sun felt so good to me that I recall thinking, "How secure and loved it must have made Betty feel." Perhaps it helped her to find her way out of the darkness of her coma. (This is an interesting consideration—one that, to my knowledge, has not been researched or discussed in the literature.)

CAPTURING THE SPIRIT OF CHRISTMAS

I vividly remember the scene on entering Betty's room one mid-December morning. I remember Betty's physical appearance. She looked so tiny and frail lying in bed in her comatose state. After 3 months her right arm and leg were still suspended from traction. Her right side had slight movement, whereas her left side was rigid with nonpurposeful movements. Her hair was growing back, after having been shaved from the craniotomy. (That morning S. L. had put a flower in Betty's short hair.) She looked pretty and very peaceful.

All of the original bandages, sutures, and wound drains had been removed. Her scars and wounds were well healed, and her skin was in good condition. Betty was off the ventilator and breathing on her own. Her tracheostomy tube had been removed, and the scar was becoming less noticeable. There were IVs. Gastrostomy tube feedings were carefully regulated to ensure the proper fluid, electrolyte, and nitrogen balance. Her weight, after an initial drop, had begun to stabilize.

I can recall what Betty's room looked like and what we had done to capture the spirit of Christmas. Overhead, from the traction bars, we suspended a mobile of stars, bright Christmas ornaments, some garland, a little bit of tinsel, and a Christmas bell. I made it a special point to ring the bell whenever I entered Betty's room, as did everyone. It became a symbol of hope that one day Betty would also be able to ring the bell. Betty's family took the lead from us and announced their arrival by ringing the bell also. They became active in many aspects of Betty's care. For example, they would take turns reading to Betty, telling her stories, and playing her favorite music.

There is something about Christmas in the ICU that makes the meaning of the holiday season especially poignant. Traditionally, Christmas is a time of love, togetherness, renewal, hope, peace, and joy. Feelings of the joy and spirit of Christmas and feelings of sadness for Betty and her family were uppermost in my mind on what I will always remember as a very special day in the ICU.

THE CHRISTMAS BELL AND JOY OF AWAKENING

I was in the nurses' station checking orders on a newly admitted patient, when I heard Betty's bell ringing loudly and continuously. I wondered who had the free time to stand there and ring that bell while the rest of us were frantically running around, since the staffing was minimal. I knew that Betty's family had not arrived; S. L. was with me, and the other nurse was busily admitting the new patient. Who could be ringing that bell? It couldn't be . . . not Betty?

S. L. must have been thinking the exact same thoughts because we almost collided in Betty's doorway. Much to our amazement and delight, there was Betty gazing at the Christmas bell. She was ringing it by tapping it with her right arm, which was suspended from the traction. What a wonderful sound to hear the ringing of that bell and to know that it was Betty who was ringing it. We were all so excited, so happy! Betty was back with us. She was awake. We had hoped for it all the time. She had just been asleep for 3 long months, but now she was awake!

I will never forget the thrill of that moment and the joyful sound of the Christmas bell. That moment captures the essence of what it means to be a critical care nurse: realizing the power of hope and persistence, using all of one's energy and skill to help those in need, and caring for others with love, concern, and respect for them as individual human beings. Suddenly, at that moment, all of these things became apparent to me.

FULFILLMENT

I believe that my experiences with Betty, and many of my other past professional experiences, have taught me something extremely valuable.

Whenever I interact with patients, with their families, and with colleagues, I often think that some aspect of my professional "self" will always stay with them, just as a part of them remains with me. It is that "something," that intangible quality of life called humanized patient care which is the essence of professional nursing. Perhaps nowhere is it experienced more dramatically than in the intensive care setting, or is it expressed more perfectly than by Tennyson's words:

"I am part of all that I have met."

MEDICAL HISTORY OF BETTY C

Profile: 13-year-old girl, hit by car while returning home from school
Injuries: Severe, multiple trauma

Description	Treatment
Fractured skull Subdural hematoma	Craniotomy

Fractured R femur
Fractured R radius
  and R ulna
	Open reduction with
	  pinning; placed in
	  balanced suspension
	  traction

Ruptured spleen	Exploratory laparotomy Splenectomy

Multiple fractured ribs
Pneumothorax
  (L lung)
	Chest tubes to
	  underwater seal
	  drainage (Pleur-evac
	  suction)

Bloody urine	Cystogram (negative for
	  bladder trauma)
	  Indwelling Foley
	  catheter with
	  continuous sterile
	  normal saline and
	  Neosporin irrigation

Facial lacerations	Plastic surgery for debridement and repair
Multiple abrasions	Cleaned and dressed

Multiple contusions
  and hematomas
	Location measured and
	  recorded; areas
	  observed for increasing
	  size; ice packs applied
	  in immediate
	  posttrauma phase

Past medical history: Negative; normal childhood
Social history:

Eighth-grade student

Average intelligence

Active participant in school athletics (i.e., volleyball, softball)

Youngest of four children (other siblings: two brothers, 18 and 16 years of age; and a sister, 15 years of age)

Parents divorced during previous year

Mother has custody of two daughters; she works, full time, as sales clerk in department store

Maternal grandparents alive and well; very supportive; both families live in the same neighborhood

122 Strategies for dealing with stress

SUGGESTED READINGS

Aiken, L. H., & Henrichs, T. F. Systematic relaxation as a nursing intervention with open heart patients. *Nursing Research,* 1971, *20,* 212-217.

Jacobson, S. Stressful situations for neonatal intensive care nurses. *American Journal of Maternal Child Nursing,* 1978, *3,* 144-150.

Johnson, J. E., Rice, V. H., Fuller, S. S., & Endress, M. P. Sensory information instruction in a coping strategy and recovery from surgery. *Research in Nursing & Health,* 1978, *1*(1), 4-17.

Marcinek, M. B. Stress in the surgical patient. *American Journal of Nursing,* 1977, *77,* 1809-1811.

Minckley, B., Burrows, D., Ehrat, K., Harper, L., Jenkin, S. A., Minckley, W. F., Page, B., Schramm, D. E., & Wood, C. Myocardial infarct stress-of-transfer inventory: Development of a research tool. *Nursing Research,* 1979, *28,* 4-10.

Murray, R. L. E. Assessment of psychological status in the surgical I.C.U. patient. *Nursing Clinics of North America.* 1975, *10*(1), 69-81.

Riehl, J., & Roy, C. *Conceptual models for nursing practice.* New York: Appleton-Century-Crofts, 1974.

Selye, H. *The stress of life* (2nd ed.). New York: McGraw-Hill, 1976.

Shannon, V. I. The transfer process: An area of concern for the C.C.U. nurse. *Heart and Lung,* 1973, *2,* 364-367.

Stephenson, C. A. Stress in the critically ill patient. *American Journal of Nursing,* 1977, 77, 1806-1809.

Stone, G., Cohen, F., & Adler, N. *Health psychology,* San Francisco: Jossey-Bass, 1979.

Volicer, B. A hospital stress rating scale. *Nursing Research,* 1975, *24,* 353-359.

PART FOUR

A philosophical view of stress

CHAPTER 13

Stress and a holistic view of health for the nursing profession

Hans Selye

.The greatest challenge faced by the healing professions, and especially by the nursing profession, is to teach people how to live in a way that is in keeping with their biological nature, and yet without hurting others. I believe that this can be achieved most effectively through the development of a code of behavior that assists individuals in coping with the stress of life in our increasingly complex society.

I admit that I am prejudiced in favor of stress research because I have worked in this area ever since I wrote the first paper on the stress syndrome in 1936. I have tried to demonstrate that stress is not a vague concept, somehow related to the decline in the influence of traditional codes of behavior, dissatisfaction with the world, or the rising cost of living. Rather, it is a clearly definable, biological and medical phenomenon whose mechanisms can be objectively identified and with which individuals can cope much better once they have understood it.

STRESS

Today, everyone talks about stress, but only a few people know exactly what it is. Although I define stress as "the nonspecific response of the body to any demand made upon it," I have found it hard to convince people that the body can respond in the same manner to things as different as a painful burn and the news that you have won the jackpot of a lottery. Yet, the basic idea is simple: All of the influences and changes individuals encounter present them with the same problem, namely adaptation in the interests of continued well-being. That there should be a "nonspecific central adaptation system" in the body for this purpose is not difficult to conceive. Such a system is examined in this chapter.

Mechanisms of adaptation and the general adaption syndrome

Important in the maintenance of the body's stability is the hypothalamus-pituitary-adrenal cortex axis (Fig. 2). Whenever an individual's

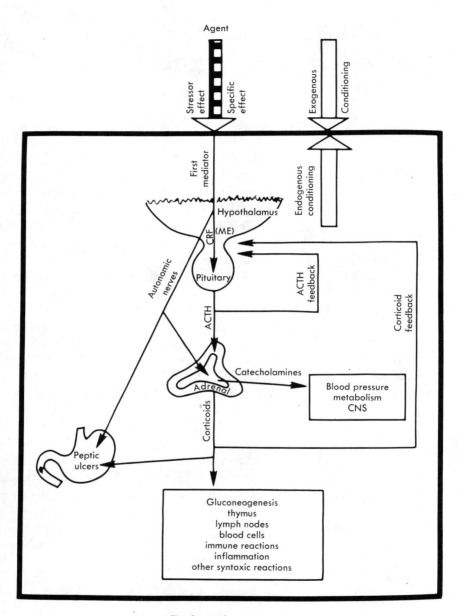

FIG. 2. For legend see opposite page.

stability is disrupted, either directly (by some physical agent) or indirectly (through individual interpretation of experience), these coordinated organs become more active in an effort to correct or improve the situation. (I say "more active" because they are never completely inactive.)

The pathways through which the information about a disrupting agent is first transmitted have not been fully clarified. Whatever its nature, this *first mediator* eventually excites the hypothalamus to produce corticotropin-releasing factor (CRF), that is, a substance or substances (endorphins, enkephalins) that stimulate the pituitary to discharge the hormone adrenocorticotropic hormone (ACTH) into the blood. ACTH, in turn, induces the external, cortical portion of the adrenal to secrete hormones that I have called *corticoids*. These elicit shrinkage of the thymus simultaneously with many other changes, such as atrophy of the lymph nodes, inhibition of inflammatory reactions, and production of sugar (a readily available source of energy). Another typical feature of the stress reaction is the development of peptic ulcers in the stomach and duodenum, a process facilitated through the increased level of corticoids in the blood and mediated in part by the autonomic nervous system.

This chain of events is cybernetically controlled by several feedback mechanisms. For instance, if there is a surplus of ACTH, a short-loop feedback returns some of it to the hypothalamus-pituitary axis, and this shuts off further ACTH production. In addition, through a long-loop feedback a high blood level of corticoids similarly inhibits too much ACTH secretion.

Simultaneously with all these processes, another important pathway is utilized to mediate the response. Hormones such as catecholamines are liberated from the adrenal medulla to activate mechanisms of general

FIG. 2. *Principal pathways mediating the response to a stressor agent and the conditioning factors that modify its effect.* As soon as any agent acts on the body (thick outer frame of the diagram), the resulting effect will depend on three factors (broad vertical arrows pointing to the upper horizontal border of the frame). All agents possess both nonspecific stressor effects (solid part of arrow) and specific properties (interrupted part of arrow). The latter are variable and characteristic of each individual agent; they are not discussed here other than to state that they are inseparably attached to the stressor effect and invariably modify it. The other two heavy vertical arrows pointing toward the upper border of the frame represent exogenous and endogenous conditioning factors that largely determine the reactivity of the body. It is clear that since all stressors have some specific effects, they cannot elicit exactly the same response in all organs. Furthermore, even the same agent will act differently in different individuals, depending on the internal and external conditioning factors that determine their reactivity. (From Selye, H. *Stress in health and disease*, Reading, Mass.: Butterworths, 1976.)

usefulness for adaptation. Adrenaline, in particular, is secreted to make available energy, to accelerate the pulse rate, to elevate blood pressure and the rate of blood circulation in the muscles, and to stimulate the central nervous system (CNS). The blood coagulation system is also enhanced by this hormone, as a protection against excessive bleeding if injuries are sustained in the encounter with the agent, event, or situation that initiated the adaptive reaction.

Innumerable other hormonal and chemical changes during adaptation check and balance the body's functioning and stability, constituting a virtual arsenal of weapons by which the organism defends itself. For example, the level of somatotropic or growth hormone (STH) may rise, and changes may occur in the output of thyroid hormones of the ovary or testis.

Regardless of the specific natures of the demand and response, however, the work required of the body is the same: to preserve *homeostasis,* the harmonious balance of the organism, through compensatory adjustments. It is the performing of this work that constitutes the state or condition I have labeled "biologic stress." The agents or demands are referred to as *stressors.* As was seen earlier, stressors are not exclusively physical in nature. Judgments and appraisals, which in the case of human beings can be highly abstract, also call forth the changes characteristic of the stress syndrome.

All of the changes in the body during stress, taken together, form what is called the *general adaptation syndrome* (GAS), which develops in three stages as follows:

1. *Alarm reaction.* The alarm reaction occurs on sudden exposure to any stimulus to which the organism is not adapted. The reaction has two phases: (a) *Shock phase,* the initial and immediate reaction to the agent; tachycardia, loss of muscle tone, and decreased temperature and blood pressure are typical symptoms, as well as the observable signs mentioned earlier. The body's resistance is diminished and, if the demand is severe, as in the case of severe burns or extremes of temperature, death will result. (b) *Countershock phase,* a rebound reaction marked by the mobilization of the defensive forces. (Most of the acute stress diseases correspond with these two phases of the alarm reaction.)

2. *Stage of resistance.* The resistance stage develops only if successful adaptation is achieved. The bodily signs of the alarm reaction have almost disappeared as increased adaptive responses handle the situation.

3. *Stage of exhaustion.* Surprisingly, resistance cannot be maintained indefinitely; if the demand is severe and prolonged, the signs of

the alarm reaction reappear, but now they are irreversible and the individual dies.

Adaptation energy

The triphasic nature of the GAS gave the first biological indication that the body's adaptability, or *adaptation energy*, is finite. Apparently, exposure to stressors can be tolerated for only so long. Investigators still do not know precisely what this energy is, but it is not caloric, since when given food the body is still unable to resist indefinitely. After exhaustion from excessively stressful activity, sleep and rest can restore resistance and adaptability almost to previous levels, but the emphasis here is on the word "almost." It would seem that, just as any machine eventually wears out even if it has enough fuel, so the human body sooner or later becomes the victim of intense or unremitting vital activity.

The stages of the GAS are analogous to the three stages of a person's life: childhood (with its characteristic low resistance and excessive responses to any kind of stimulation); adulthood (during which adaptation to most commonly encountered agents has occurred and resistance is increased); and finally, senility (characterized by irreversible loss of adaptability and eventual exhaustion ending with death). Indeed, it is intriguing to speculate that *aging* may be an extended GAS, or, if you prefer, the GAS, as observed here, represents a process of *accelerated aging*.

Special effects and conditioning factors

At this point it will be helpful to discuss two apparent objections to accepting the concept of a single, stereotyped response to stress.

1. Qualitatively different agents of equal toxicity or stressor potency do not necessarily elicit exactly the same reactions in different people. The effects specific to any given agent usually modify the effects and manifestations of the general stress syndrome. (Thus it took many years to recognize and prove the existence of the latter.)

2. The same degree of stress, induced by the same agent, may produce different effects and even lesions in different individuals. The fact that the state of stress, even if due to the same agent, can cause different effects in different individuals has been traced to "conditioning factors," which can selectively enhance or inhibit one or the other stress effect. This conditioning may be endogenous (genetic predisposition, age, or sex) or exogenous (treatment with certain hormones, drugs, or dietary factors). Under the influence of such conditioning factors, a nor-

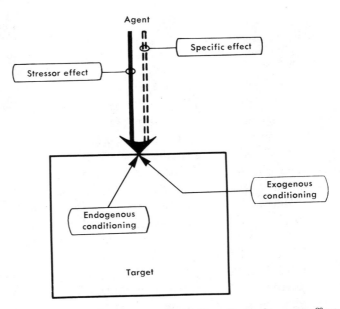

FIG. 3. Any agent has both stressor and specific effects. Stressor effects are non-specific by definition, being common to diverse stimuli, whereas specific effects are variable and characteristic of each individual agent. The response, however, does not depend exclusively on these two actions of the agent; the reactivity of the target also plays a role, which can be modified by numerous internal or external conditioning (predisposing or protective) factors. Thus it is clear that since all stressor agents have some specific effects, they cannot always elicit exactly the same response, and even the same agent will always act differently in different individuals, depending on the internal and external conditioning factors that determine the reactivity of the terrain.

mally well-tolerated degree of stress can even become pathogenic. It can selectively affect those parts of the body which are particularly sensitized both by these conditioning factors and by the specific effects of the eliciting agent, just as physical tensions of equal strength in different chains will break the particular link that is the weakest as a result of internal or external factors (Fig. 3).

Diseases of adaptation

In general, the hormonal and other responses of stress, just outlined, aid adaptation to environmental change or stimuli. They are sometimes the cause of disease, however, especially if the state of stress is prolonged or intense. These "diseases of adaptation" or "stress diseases" are due to insufficient, excessive, or faulty reactions to stressors. Nevertheless, just as there is no pure stressor, that is, an agent which causes only the non-specific response and has no specific action, so there are no pure diseases of adaptation. The stress mechanism participates in the pathogenesis of every malady, but no disease is due to nonspecific factors alone. The justification for placing a malady into this category is directly proportional to the importance of the role that maladjustment to stress plays in its development. In some instances, for example, surgical shock, stress may be by far the most important pathogenic factor. In other cases, such as instantly lethal intoxications, traumatic injuries to the spinal cord, or most congenital malformations, it plays little or no role, either because the damage is inflicted so rapidly that there is no time for any adaptive process or because the pathogen is highly specific. In the latter event any stress-related effect is a secondary and not the primary component.

Some common stress diseases are high blood pressure, cardiac accidents, gastric or duodenal ulcers (the "stress ulcers"), and various types of mental disturbances.

As I have said before, there is no disease that can be attributed exclusively to maladaptation; the cause of nonspecific responses will always be modified by various "conditioning factors" that enhance, diminish, or otherwise alter disease susceptibility. Most important among these are the specific effect of the primary pathogen and the factors influencing the body's reactivity by endogenous or exogenous conditioners. Hence, the diseases of adaptation cannot be ascribed to any one pathogen but only to "pathogenic constellations"; they belong to what has been called the pluricausal diseases (multifactorial maladies), which depend on the simultaneous effect of several factors that alone would not produce disease.

A NEW CONCEPT OF HEALTH

From the foregoing it should be evident that psychological factors can often be the decisive influence both in the causation of disease and in the course taken by an established disorder. In fact, this is where the profession of nursing can make a special contribution, since its practitioners are in direct control of such variables. Yet it would be an error to think that a clear distinction can always be made between physical and mental causes of stress; for example, anticipation of physical trauma can be a psychic stressor, as anyone who has ever required surgery will understand. What is really needed are principles for general stress management that would ensure homeostasis on all levels.

Today's medical and nursing practice, at least in the West, has only just started to explore the close interrelation of body and mind. Yet the goal of medicine should be to understand the patient as a person, to establish the circumstances that precipitated his illness, the underlying conflicts, hostilities, and griefs—in short, the bruised nature of his emotional state. The modern physician ought to know as much about emotions and thoughts as about disease symptoms and drugs. This approach would appear to hold more promise of cure than anything that medicine has given the human race to date.

Clearly the field of stress has much to offer in this regard. The degree to which homeostasis, the basic determinant of health, is an issue of the total organism, of consciousness as well as physical existence, becomes apparent when one considers the following facts which emerge from stress theory: (1) that the aspects of life requiring adaptation, that is, calling forth the organic stress reaction and initiating the GAS, are not merely composed of matter but often can be grasped only in terms of concepts or, if you will, mental states (e.g., one's "life situation"); and (2) that these nonmaterial demands can disrupt homeostasis in two ways, either by being simply beyond a person's power of adaptability or by causing diseases of adaptation because there is a particularly "weak link" in the structure of the person's organism.

This view of health and disease, then, is that they are not merely individual interactions between pathogens and human beings but they involve, rather, the entire spectrum of other relationships, including those with one's spouse, employer, children, neighbors, and spiritual or medical advisers. Too much consideration has been directed toward specific pathogens and toward specific disease models and not enough toward the patient and how he developed his particular disease. Only when health professionals shift their focus from diseased parts to the whole being, can they learn more about what activates the adaptation syndrome at all levels within the organism and understand why stress affects different people in different ways.

The integrating concept of health as a question of body, mind, and spirit is assuming phenomenal popularity and importance. This holistic approach aims at enhancing an individual's total well-being, in part through self-awareness. By learning to gauge one's own innate energy, and potential weaknesses and strengths, everyone can benefit from this approach. True, it requires a great deal of self-discipline and willpower, but society must not lose sight of the vital awareness that each individual is responsible for his or her own health and well-being. Otherwise people will continue to be plagued by stress-induced diseases.

Humans have always been preoccupied with their health and have wanted to improve it, both the mind and the body. Throughout history, innumerable great thinkers have approached the problem from the points of view of theology, psychology, sociology, and particularly, medicine. But whatever the approach or technique they favored, the focus was always specialized. Only now are health professionals really beginning to look on health as a holistic problem. After all, they are thinking of the health of the individual as such, and they will never arrive at a satisfactory solution if each professional takes different reductionist points of view. Individually, scientists have been successful in improving health by research limited to molecular biology, electron microscopy, pharmacology, behavioral philosophy (including religious codes), sociology, politics, economics, or any of the other specialized disciplines, but they must not look on their particular field of expertise as the only, all-encompassing solution to the troubles of human beings and the only road to happiness. There is no great point in elucidating or improving one part of the human machine if another vital part is meanwhile deteriorating and destroying the whole.

Just as wars will not be avoided by more sophisticated weaponry, so disease can never be completely eradicated merely by improvements in pharmacology, immunotherapy, or any other purely medical means.

A BIOLOGICAL CODE OF ETHICS

From what the laboratory and the clinical study of somatic diseases have taught me concerning stress, I have tried to arrive at a code of ethics based not on blind superstition, inspiration, or societal traditions but on the scientifically verifiable laws that govern the body's maintenance of homeostasis.

In my monograph *Stress without Distress,* which discussed the behavioral implications of the stress concept, and in my autobiography, I attempted to show in detail how people can adjust their personal reactions to enjoy fully the eustress of success and accomplishment without suffering the distress commonly generated by frustrating friction and purposeless, aggressive behavior against their surroundings.

For example, it helps a great deal to understand the fundamental advantages and disadvantages of what I call "catatoxic" and "syntoxic" responses. Research has shown that to resist different toxic stressors the body can regulate its reactions through chemical messengers and nervous stimuli, which either pacify or incite to fight. The syntoxic stimuli act as tissue tranquilizers, creating a state of passive tolerance that permits a kind of symbiosis or peaceful coexistence with aggressors. The catatoxic agents, on the other hand, cause chemical changes (mainly through the production of hepatic microsomal enzymes) that lead to an active attack on the pathogen, usually by accelerating its metabolic degradation.

Applied to everyday problems, this understanding should lead to choices most likely to provide individuals with the pleasant stress of fulfillment and victory, thereby avoiding the self-destructive distress of failure and frustration. With regard to interpersonal relations, this means that each person must live without creating unnecessary conflicts with others. Such an approach, besides ensuring peace of mind and body, earns the goodwill, respect, and even love of others, thereby providing the highest degree of security.

In *Stress without Distress* I illustrate this possibility by an example taken from daily life that shows how diseases can be produced indirectly by inappropriate or excessive adaptive reactions. When you meet a helpless drunk who showers you with insults but is obviously unable to do you any harm, nothing will happen if you take a syntoxic attitude — go past and ignore him. However, if you respond catatoxically and fight, or even only prepare to fight, the consequences may be tragic. You will discharge catecholamines that increase blood pressure and pulse rate while your whole nervous system will become alarmed and tense in anticipation of combat. If you happen to be a coronary candidate, the result may be a fatal brain hemorrhage or coronary accident. In this case, who is the murderer? The drunk did not even touch you. This is biological suicide! Death was caused by choosing the wrong reaction. If, on the other hand, the man who showers you with insults is a homicidal maniac with a dagger in his hand, evidently determined to kill you, you must take an aggressive catatoxic attitude. You must try to disarm him, even at the calculated risk of injury to yourself from the physical accompaniments of the alarm reaction in preparation for a fight. Contrary to common opinion, it is clear that Nature does not always know best because on both the cellular and the interpersonal level, people do not always recognize what is and what is not worth fighting for.

The policy of hoarding the goodwill of one's neighbor is often followed implicitly by many, since it is merely a reflection of the deep-rooted instinct of humans and even of other animals to collect. My guideline merely attempts to direct a natural impulse of acquisition toward what I consider the most permanent and valuable commodity people can accumulate: a huge capital of goodwill that protects them against attacks by their fellow humans.

"Love they neighbor as thyself," one of the oldest maxims for purpose and conduct, was propounded to please God and thereby offer security to the human race. Since philosophy is based on natural laws, it is perhaps not surprising that for centuries, throughout the world, this and many others of its elements have turned up again and again in the most diverse religions and political doctrines, although the people in whose cultures these elements appeared were often unrelated and may not even have known of each other's existence.

Usually, however, their doctrines were supported by mysticism and blind trust in someone's infallibility rather than by scientific investigation. In this age it is time to update the guideline by rephrasing it to *"Earn* thy neighbor's love"; in this form it is biologically sound. Moreover, it cannot conflict with any religion or philosophy; ardent believers in any doctrine can use this code to complement their own. It provides scientific support for some of the most deep-rooted and generally accepted precepts of the fellowship of the human race.

Nature is the fountainhead of all human problems and solutions; the closer people keep to her the more they will realize that, despite the apparently enormous divergences in interpretation and explanation, her laws have always prevailed and can never become obsolete. The realization of this truth is most likely to convince everyone that, in a sense, not only all humans but all living beings are brothers and sisters. To avoid the stress of conflict, frustration, and hate, to achieve peace and happiness, scientists should devote more attention to a better understanding of the natural basis of human motivation and behavior.

The whole translation of the laws governing resistance of cells and organs into a code of ethics comes down to the following three precepts:

1. *Find your own stress level.* People differ with regard to the amount and kind of work they consider worth doing to meet the exigencies of daily life and assure their future security and happiness. In this respect, everyone is influenced by hereditary predispositions and the expectations of their society. Only through planned self-analysis can individuals establish what they really want; many people suffer all their lives because they are too conservative to risk a radical change and break with tradition.

2. *Altruistic egoism.* The selfish hoarding of the goodwill, respect, esteem, support, and love of one's neighbor is the most efficient way to utilize pent-up energy and create enjoyable, beautiful, or useful things.

3. EARN *thy neighbor's love.* This motto, unlike the command to love, is compatible with the natural structure of human beings. Who would blame him who wants to assure his own homeostasis and happi-

ness only by accumulating the treasure of other people's benevolence toward him? Such a desire transforms unavoidable selfishness into unselfishness, and everyone benefits.

What it comes down to is this:

Fight for your highest attainable aim
But do not put up resistance in vain.

SUGGESTED READINGS

Goldwag, E. (Ed.). *Inner balance: The power of holistic healing.* Englewood Cliffs, N.J.: Prentice-Hall, 1979.

Knowles, J. H. (Ed.). *Doing better and feeling worse: Health in the United States.* New York: W. W. Norton, 1977.

Ng, L., & Davis, D. L. (Eds.). *Strategies for public health.* New York: Van Nostrand-Reinhold, in press.

Selye, H. *Stress without distress.* Philadelphia: J. B. Lippincott, 1974.

Selye, H. *The stress of life* (2nd ed.). New York: McGraw-Hill, 1976.

Selye, H. *Coping with stress in 1979.* In *1979 information please almanac.* New York: Information Please, 1979.

Selye, H. *Stress in health and disease.* Reading, Mass.: Butterworths, 1979.

Selye, H. *The stress of my life* (2nd ed.). New York: Van Nostrand-Reinhold, 1979.

Wolf, S., & Goodell, H. *Behavioral science in clinical medicine.* Springfield, Ill.: Charles C Thomas, 1976.

Stress-reduction training modules for nurses

James W. Grout

The stress-reduction training modules for nurses are arranged in the following order:

Category of stressor	Modules
Physical and mental fatigue	Module 1: Exercise Module 2: Stress and health Module 3: Relaxation response and techniques Module 4: Massage and touch
Interpersonal relationships	Module 5: Communication skills Module 6: Assertiveness Module 7: Group process Module 8: Conflict resolution
Nature of direct patient care	Module 9: Crisis intervention Module 10: Problem solving Module 11: Death and dying Module 12: Ethics
Management of the unit	Module 13: Management of the unit
Inadequate knowledge and skills	Module 14: Inadequate knowledge and skills
Physical work environment	Module 15: Physical work environment

Module 1: Exercise

By its very nature, the ICU presents the nurse who works there with a series of crises that, unless followed by some compensatory relaxation, can lead to a condition of chronic stress. Usually one can contend with a stressful situation; it is encountered, dealt with, and followed by a period of relaxation. This coping response can be thwarted, however, if a second stressful situation intervenes. Rather than returning to a prestress level, the original stress is compounded and, eventually, becomes chronic and unresolved. This pattern *can* be broken. Sometimes, your body does it for you by becoming sick. It is much better, of course, that your stress be managed before that happens. One way is by exercise. Not only will exercise help you to be more physically fit, and so better able to cope with stress, but a psychological stance is taken as well when you deliberately put aside time in your life to exercise and demonstrate self-care.

Some exercises can be done at work, with the advantage that their effect will be felt immediately. Stretching is one of the simplest ways to relax the muscles that contract during stress. You should be careful, however, not to stretch more than is comfortable. Concentrate on the particular muscles being stretched until you feel them begin to pull and then hold that position for several seconds. Remember, though, that they are not to hurt. It may be that from one session to another you stretch no more than a fraction of an inch. Whatever stretching you do, whether it is toe touching, side bends, or neck circling, do it slowly and deliberately.

Isometric exercises, which contract the muscle without any joint movement, are another unobtrusive way to promote circulation and induce the automatic relaxation of a muscle that occurs after it has contracted. Cardiopulmonary fitness and its attendant feeling of well-being derive from a different type of exercise, however. Aerobic exercises such as running, swimming, cycling, and even walking may have to be done away from work but can have a profound effect on the way you feel when you *are* there. You may find that your diet and sleeping habits change as well. Several studies (Eliot, Forker, & Robertson, 1976; Greist, Klein, Eischens, Faris, Gurman, & Morgan, 1979; Solomon & Bumpus, 1978) have even indicated the benefits of running in lessening stress and depression. Although activity such as jogging undoubtedly has beneficial results, it also should be enjoyable in itself. Because it should be fun, pay attention to those physiological signs (soreness, lowered resistance, chronic fatigue) which may indicate that you are pushing yourself too hard. Cooper (1977) suggests a satisfactory level of cardiopulmonary fitness for women under 30 years of age, as measured by oxygen consumption, to be 36 ml/kg/min, a level to which he assigns 24 points per week and which can be achieved by a number of exercise programs, for example, jogging 1.5 miles in 13.5 minutes four times a week.

It is important to remember that such a level of fitness should be attained only gradually, and Cooper outlines suitable 10-week programs for a number of exercises. More specific remarks about women running are provided by Ullyot (1976). Some general hints should be kept in mind, however. Regular, almost daily, activity that follows a pattern of alternating hard and easy workouts and emphasizes distance over speed is best. Although you will have your own natural running style, try to land heel first or flat-footed. Remember to warm up, either by jogging the first few minutes very slowly and easily or, better, by some stretching exercises, especially of the hamstrings.

The emphasis of this unit, more than the specific exercise programs themselves, is that you exercise. You may exercise already, even if you simply roll your head to reduce the tension in your neck, and if you do not exercise, you know that you should. This is to remind you that by doing so, you can not only reduce the stress of work but begin, at the most basic level, a program of stress reduction which will give you a greater sense of well-being and control over yourself and your environment.

REFERENCES

Cooper, K. H. *The aerobics way.* New York: Bantam Books, 1977.

Eliot, R. S., Forker, A. D., & Robertson, R. J. Aerobic exercise as a therapeutic modality in the relief of stress. *Advances in Cardiology,* 1976, *18,* 231-242.

Greist, J. H., Klein, M. H., Eischens, R. R., Faris, J., Gurman, A. S., & Morgan, W. P. Running as treatment for depression. *Comprehensive Psychiatry,* 1979, *20,* 41-54.

Solomon, E. G., & Bumpus, A. K. The running meditation response: An adjunct to psychotherapy. *American Journal of Psychotherapy,* 1978, *32,* 583-592.

Ullyot, J. *Women running.* Mountain View, Calif.: World Publications, 1976.

Module 2: Stress and health

Together with exercise, proper diet and rest are basic to good health. Eating more whole grains and fresh fruit and fewer processed foods and decreasing the intake of refined sugars and fats will have a synergistic effect on your management of stress: You will feel better and so be less susceptible to the stressors of work, which should make you feel better still. Pay attention, too, not only to what you eat but to where, when, and why you eat as well. Remember that the same pleasant, relaxed feeling which comes from eating can also derive from jogging and meditation.

VITAMINS

Vitamins cannot be made by the body but must be supplied by what you eat. Although a well-balanced diet should provide most necessary vitamins and minerals, individual requirements differ and, under certain circumstances, may have to be increased to compensate for greater rates of utilization and excretion. Certain B-complex vitamins, for example, as well as vitamin C, are depleted under conditions of stress and with oral contraceptive use. Oral contraceptives, especially, can alter the body's requirement of several vitamins and minerals (Larsson-Cohn, 1975; Theuer, 1972). There is an increased need for vitamins B_6 and C and a probable need for increased intakes of folic acid and vitamin B_{12}, vitamin B_2, and zinc. To compensate for such deficiencies, the requirements for vitamins B_6 and C may have to be as much as ten times the recommended daily allowance for adult women, that is, 20 to 30 mg of B_6 and 450 mg or more, of C. Because these requirements can be aggravated by poor nutrition, it is important that you be particularly aware of your diet when you are stressed.

SUGAR, SALT, AND CHOLESTEROL

The individual consumption of refined sugar in the United States is now well over 100 pounds a year. Aside from the obvious amounts in desserts, soft drinks, and breakfast cereals (e.g., a 12-ounce soft drink contains approximately 2 tablespoons of sugar, and even most bran and "natural" cereals are 10% to 25% sugar), sugar is added to many other commercial products to enhance their flavor. Not only does sugar promote tooth decay and increase the blood level of insulin but it also provides calories that are completely empty of any vitamins and minerals.

The refined carbohydrates in toast and jam or a pastry for breakfast are digested and absorbed much more rapidly, for example, than more wholesome food that could be utilized by the body over a period of several hours. As a result, when this source of quick energy has been depleted, your body is left without adequate energy to meet its needs, and the level of blood glucose may be even lower than it was before you ate. After the initial rush of sugar, you again feel without energy. Eating enough carbohydrates to satisfy your hunger also provides far more calories than can be utilized, and whatever is not used is stored as fat (Robertson, Flinders, & Godfrey, 1976). You already know this and have heard it before, but: *Eat a good breakfast.*

Like sugar, salt often is added commercially to foods, especially in convenience or snack foods. The sodium in salt, however, is a key element in regulating fluid balance in the body and can, with excessive and prolonged intake, lead to hypertension. Since the basic American diet already contains more salt than is needed by the body to replace what normally is excreted, salt should be used sparingly in cooking and not at all at the table.

Some cholesterol in the blood not only is natural but essential. When more cholesterol is taken in than is needed, for example, the liver makes less. More cholesterol in the blood, however, than can be regulated may increase the risk of atherosclerosis. Such a risk may be aggravated further by emotional stress. Try, then, to lessen your blood cholesterol level by eating fewer eggs (not more than three or four a week) and avoid foods that are high in butterfat, such as butter, cheese, and cream.

SLEEP

Ulene (1978) offers some suggestions for a restful night's sleep, which usually means 7 or 8 hours. His suggestions for getting to sleep more quickly, sleeping more soundly, and waking more refreshed are as follows:

- Don't go to bed unless you are sleepy, and when you are sleepy, go to bed.
- If you eat before bedtime, let it be a light snack, and avoid stimulants such as coffee, tea, and cola drinks (even smoking).
- Exercises should be stretching or isometric, since they cause the muscles to relax totally afterward.
- If there is any unresolved business or conflict, try to resolve it before going to bed.

As Felton (1975) has indicated, body rhythms such as temperature and blood pressure normally tend to rise in the morning, reach a high between noon and late afternoon or early evening, begin to fall, and reach their low point between 2 and 5 A.M. People are used to sleeping when many body rhythms are at their low point in the cycle. Altering the pattern of sleeping and waking can affect this sequence (as any of you who work shift rotation already know). Not only do temporal referents change for the nurse on the night shift but temperature, body cycles, and excretion patterns change as well over a period of a week or so while the body adjusts to the new schedule. It is because these various physiological rhythms adjust at different rates that a change in shift from day or night and back again results in some initial loss of synchronization. Since biological rhythms are associated with such temporal fluctuations, nurses who are beginning a new shift should remind themselves that efficiency and performance will be affected and that errors are most likely to occur at the low point of their cycle, when many physiological and psychological functions normally are at rest.

REFERENCES

Felton, G. Body rhythm effects on rotating work shifts. *Journal of Nursing Administration,* 1975, 5(2), 16-19.

Larsson-Cohn, U. Oral contraceptives and vitamins: A review. *American Journal of Obstetrics and Gynecology,* 1975, *121,* 84-90.

Robertson, L., Flinders, C., & Godfrey, B. *Laurel's kitchen: A handbook for vegetarian cookery and nutrition.* Petaluma, Calif.: Nilgiri Press, 1976.

Theuer, R. C. Effects of oral contraceptive agents on vitamin and mineral needs: A review. *Journal of Reproductive Medicine,* 1972, *8,* 13-19.

Ulene, A. *Feeling fine.* New York: Ballantine Books, 1978.

Module 3: Relaxation response and techniques

Because there is a relationship between psychological and physiological change, techniques that relax the mind can relax the body as well, and vice versa. Either by eliciting the relaxation response or by practicing other relaxation techniques such as progressive relaxation, autogenic training, guided imagery, and breathing exercises, you should be better able to relax your mind *and* your body.

RELAXATION RESPONSE

In a way, the body is naive and really cannot distinguish between the stress induced by a genuinely threatening situation and the common daily stressors of work. Its response to both is one of "flight or fight." What Benson (1975) has called the "relaxation response" is the physiological opposite to this reaction and is characterized by decreased sympathetic nervous system activity, for example, a decrease in oxygen consumption, carbon dioxide elimination, heart and respiratory rate, and blood pressure. In a study of the relaxation response on five self-reported measures of health, performance, and well-being, the greatest mean improvement on every index occurred among those who had been taught a technique for producing the relaxation response (Peters, Benson, & Porter, 1977).

The relaxation response can be elicited in a variety of ways, among them Transcendental Meditation and certain practices of Zen Buddhism. One of the simplest, however, is that developed by Benson. The following comprise the four components to his technique:

1. *A quiet environment.* The environment should be quiet and without distractions, since sounds, even background noise, can be distracting and prevent the response from occurring.

2. *Decreased muscle tonus.* To reduce muscle tension, sit in a comfortable chair in as restful position as possible. The head and arms may be supported and the feet propped up, if desired. Tight-fitting clothing should be loosened. Your eyes should remain closed throughout the practice.

3. *A passive attitude.* You should relax and not worry about your performance. Distracting thoughts simply should be disregarded and attention redirected to the technique.

4. *A mental device.* To free yourself from logical, externally oriented thought, focus on a single-syllable word or sound, which is repeated silently or audibly.

To elicit the relaxation response, sit quietly in a comfortable and private place. Close your eyes and relax all your muscles, beginning at the feet and progressing up to the face. While slowly exhaling through your nose, silently say the syllable or word that you have chosen. (Benson suggests the word "one" because of its simplicity and neutrality; you could use "om" or any other mantra.) Remain passive and concentrate on the sound of the word, allowing the response to occur naturally. Continue this practice for 15 to 20 minutes, then wait several minutes after meditating before opening your eyes. The relaxation response should be practiced once or, preferably, twice daily, usually before breakfast and dinner, although for many individuals this may be more practice than is necessary. Fewer than three practice periods a week, however, produce little physiological change.

PROGRESSIVE RELAXATION

Because the automatic response of a muscle to contraction is relaxation, one simple way to relax a muscle is to contract it first. In progressive relaxation, developed by Jacobson (1978), the muscles are systematically contracted and relaxed.

Begin by lying down, with your arms at your sides and your legs stretched out. Lie still for several minutes, with your eyes closed, and relax.

- With your palm down, slowly and steadily bend your hand back at the wrist until you feel tension at the upper part of your forearm muscles. After being aware of this sensation for a minute or so, release your hand and allow it to drop back to your side. Repeat.
- Now with your palm up, bend your hand toward you until you can feel tension in the lower part of your forearm muscles. Relax and repeat.
- Bend your foot toward you until you feel tension in the muscles along your shins. Relax and repeat.
- Extend your foot away from you until you feel tension in the calf. Relax and repeat.

These exercises should make you much more aware of the sensation of relaxation in your arms and legs. The process of tensing and then relaxing the muscles can be repeated for other parts of the body: Tense, be aware of the tension, relax.

AUTOGENIC TRAINING

Developed by Schultz (Luthe, 1963), autogenic training is based on the principle that psychological and physiological change are intimately related. By concentrating, for instance, on the warmth of your fingers and suggesting to yourself that they are getting heavier and warmer and more filled with blood, it is actually possible to increase their temperature. Such control of the autonomic nervous system, however, involves considerable time and practice—more, perhaps, than you can give. For this reason autogenic training is simply suggested here as a means of relaxing that you may want to pursue further. There are relaxation or warmth phrases that you can repeat two or three times while you relax quietly with your eyes closed: "I am beginning to feel relaxed (or warm) . . . My feet feel heavy and relaxed . . . My ankles (knees, hips), feel heavy and relaxed." Phrases such as these also can be used for other parts of the body.

GUIDED IMAGERY

Ulene (1978) reviews some of the different relaxation techniques, one of which is guided imagery. Because the mind responds almost as well to symbolic stimuli as it does to actual stimuli, this technique can be an effective means of reducing stress. By visualizing, for example, a quiet scene, it is possible for you to become more tranquil yourself, almost as if it were actually being experienced.

Find a private place where you can sit comfortably for several minutes. Close your eyes, relax, and breathe deeply through your nose. Imagine a scene that is especially restful to you, perhaps a place that you have been on vacation or one where you would like to visit, such as a sunny tropical beach or a pastoral farm setting. Visualize not only the scenery but imagine the sounds and smells as well. Enjoy this imagery for several minutes, then slowly open your eyes.

BREATHING

When you are not stressed, your breathing will be slow, deep, and regular. To ensure that it remains that way, Ulene suggests several breathing exercises. They should be done in a quiet environment while you are sitting comfortably in a chair, unrestricted by tight clothing. Remember to breathe in through your nose. When you inhale, expand your ribs and push your abdomen out; when you exhale, pull the abdomen in. This is similar to breathing in yoga but is just the opposite of how we usually breathe.

- Close your eyes and concentrate on your breathing. Exhale comfortably, pulling your abdomen in. Now inhale rapidly, taking as much air into your lungs as you can and filling your entire rib cage. Draw in your abdomen, forcing the accumulated air out through your mouth. Repeat ten times.
- This time, inhale slowly so that the breath you draw in is held for 5

seconds. Hold for another 5 seconds and then exhale slowly until your lungs are completely empty. Repeat five times.

REFERENCES

Benson, H. *The relaxation response.* New York: Avon Books, 1975.

Jacobson, E. *You must relax* (5th ed.). New York: McGraw-Hill, 1978.

Luthe, W. Autogenic training, method, research and application in medicine. *American Journal of Psychotherapy,* 1963, *17,* 174-195.

Peters, R. K., Benson, H., & Porter, D. Daily relaxation response breaks in a working population: 1. Effects on self-reported measures of health, performance, and well-being. *American Journal of Public Health,* 1977, *67,* 946-953.

Ulene, A. *Feeling fine.* New York: Ballantine Books, 1978.

Module 4: Massage and touch

Muscles contract in response to the electrochemical stimulation of brain impulses. Usually, this contraction is required for physical movement, but in many stressful situations, although no movement occurs, the muscles still contract in anticipation that it may occur. If stress continues, this tension can become sustained at increasingly higher levels without any return to a prestress level of relaxation.

MASSAGE

One of the most direct and pleasant ways of lessening muscle tension is by massage (Downing, 1972). Although it is nicer to be massaged by another person, you can do it yourself just as easily. Often there is considerable muscle tension in the neck and shoulders, and massage of these areas is especially helpful in reducing tension. You may want to experiment, however, with a less familiar form of massage called *shiatsu* or acupressure (Ohashi, 1976).

In Oriental philosophy the energy of the body is thought to be channeled through the body along invisible conduits called meridian lines. Along these lines are particular points (*tsubo*) where nerves hurt when the flow of energy through them is blocked. Pressure on these sensitive points (which in *shiatsu* is administered by the fingers as opposed to needles in acupuncture) frees this blockage. Although connected by the meridian lines, the location of the *tsubo* is not the same as the source of the complaint but may be quite removed from it. Tiredness, for example, is thought to be alleviated by pressing hard with the thumb at a point (*ro kyu*) between where the tips of the flexed middle and ring fingers touch the crease of the palm.

More general *shiatsu* techniques include the following:
- At the point (*a mon*) of the indentation of the neck just above the hairline (between the first and second vertebrae), press hard three times in an upward direction for 5 seconds.
- Placing your hands on the back of the neck, with your fingers intertwined, squeeze your palms together to massage the neck.

Because of the great concentration of nerves in the feet, foot massage is also helpful in reducing tension. Even if you do not press specific points of the foot, general massage can be relaxing.

TOUCH

The sensation of being touched is one to which human beings respond even before birth and one which is fundamental in the later development of behavior (Montagu, 1978). Caring and involvement are conveyed through touch as well as the associations invested in touch by experience. One survey (Barnett, 1972) found that the ICU was among the units where therapeutic touch was most frequently utilized in patient care. Touch can be just as beneficial in situations where it is shared between nurses themselves.

REFERENCES

Barnett, K. A study of the current utilization of touch by health team personnel with hospitalized patients. *International Journal of Nursing Studies,* 1972, *9,* 195-209.

Downing, G. *The massage book.* New York: Random House, 1972.

Montagu, A. *Touching* (2nd ed.). New York: Harper & Row, 1978.

Ohashi, W. *Do-it-yourself shiatsu: How to perform the ancient Japanese art of "acupuncture without needles."* New York: E. P. Dutton, 1976.

Module 5: Communication skills

"Do you mean what you say or do you say what you mean?" This quote from Lewis Carroll's *Alice in Wonderland* sums up the difficulty of effective communication. Yet no other aspect of interpersonal relationships is so important. In the ICU it is often critical. Although communication can be by virtually any means that conveys information to another, whether or not it is effective depends on those data being understood. Some suggestions follow to help you communicate more effectively.

The greatest problem in effective communication is its illusion. Often, what you thought was clearly expressed has been completely misunderstood. Frequently, it is not even possible for you to discover that mistaken impression until later; even worse, you may never realize it. Such confusion usually occurs because the speaker was not clear or the listener was not attentive or both failed to make certain that they had understood each another.

Obviously, a sense of credibility and trust enhances understanding. There is less suspicion, and communication is regarded as it should be: an open and honest attempt to convey information. Because there is a possibility, however, for misunderstanding even in a trusting relationship, you should not only try to be as understandable as possible, that is, clear and specific, but make certain that you *have* been understood. This can be discovered most readily simply by asking if you have and by being attentive to other, nonverbal gestures, such as a quizzical expression, which might indicate that you have not.

Rogers (Claus & Bailey, 1977) has suggested that verbal responses can be characterized as one of five types: evaluative, interpretative, supportive, probing, or understanding. All of them, as their labels suggest, indicate the ways in which the listener interacts with, and responds to, the remarks of another. You may want to keep them in mind during your next conversation as a reminder of how well you are communicating. When the listener interprets your comments, does it indicate, for example, that you have been heard correctly? Or does an evaluative or probing statement reveal that you may not have expressed yourself as you intended? A supportive response would indicate that you had, an understanding, or paraphrasing, one would indicate that you might not have and that more information is necessary.

Speaking precisely or listening carefully is not easy. Often, in formulating a response, one does not always listen to what has been said or listens to details instead of the essential message. Such selective perception, although often necessary, does allow for misunderstanding. It can be reduced, however, if you are as unambiguous and specific in your statements as possible. Depending on the response of the listener, you should be able to determine how well you are communicating.

REFERENCE

Claus, K. E., & Bailey, J. T. *Power and influence in health care: A new approach to leadership.* St. Louis: C. V. Mosby, 1977.

Module 6: Assertiveness

One aspect of work in the ICU that has been found to be most satisfying for the nurse is interpersonal relationships. It is also one of the least satisfying. Given the complexity of human interaction, this apparent contradiction is not surprising. A possible reason for it, however, may be. Individual self-assertion, probably more than any other skill, can determine the effectiveness and satisfaction of interpersonal relationships and may be one reason why they are regarded so differently. To be inhibited, for instance, by anxiety in such relationships, or to have responsibility for patient care but not the authority for it, or even to be uncertain about whether that responsibility is to be directed to the patient, to the physician, or to both are all real conflicts which can partially be helped by assertiveness training.

Assertive behavior (e.g., Alberti & Emmons, 1978; Jakubowski-Spector, 1973; Rathus, 1975) allows the affirmation of oneself without denying the rights of others. It means the honest, direct, and appropriate expression of one's feelings, beliefs, and opinions but not at the expense of another. Perhaps more than anything else, it means feeling that you have a right to such expression and affirming that others do as well. This respect both for yourself and the other person distinguishes assertive behavior from aggression, which denies the extension to others of what you expect from them. Although this difference may seem more a matter of semantics (my assertion is the other person's aggression), the distinction is real and marks the difference between behavior that is truly self-enhancing and that which is so only at the expense of another. Assertion is not feeling guilty or anxious when honest and spontaneous reactions are expressed in an appropriate manner. Lastly, it is the realization that non-assertion can be more distressing than whatever initial apprehension is felt in asserting yourself. At least, you will have made your feelings known and obliged the other person to consider them.

You are aware of those specific situations which causes you anxiety. The anger that they also may evoke is an equally natural feeling but one that is not often expressed or expressed appropriately. Your verbal message, for example, will not be effective if it is inconsistent with how you act. Eye contact is especially important in conveying the sincerity of what you are saying. Although there is no need to stare, to look away frequently from the other's gaze can indicate a lack of consonance between what you are saying and what you mean. Other social habits, such as the physical distance between you both or turning your body so that it faces the person to whom you are speaking also are important in conveying your impression, as is facial expression and tone of voice.

Much of what has been said so far has been generalizations. Many of the scenarios given in the literature, however, often seem contrived and obvious and have little in common with those interpersonal situations in the ICU which may cause you anxiety. Examples that *would* help you are best shared among yourselves. They can be practiced in several ways. One is rehearsal or role playing, which allows you to simulate problem situations and practice ways of responding to them. Coaching or feedback from others also will provide some idea as to the effectiveness of a particular assertive response. Modeling behavior can serve as a demonstration of how both parties might act in a situation. Empathy, for example, may be a more effective response to another person than overtly assertive behavior.

If specific examples have not been given here, it is because there are no easy answers to situations that, if they could be easily resolved, would not hold for you the anxiety they do. In fact, it is not so much the situation at all that is important but you and your feelings about yourself. It is you who must determine whether assertiveness would be helpful. It is simply an option that you can choose to use. Remember, though, that it is not a means simply of getting your own way. Assertiveness is expressing your feelings to others, whether they are ones of anger or affection.

REFERENCES

Alberti, R. E., & Emmons, M. L. *Your perfect right* (3rd ed.). San Luis Obispo, Calif.: Impact, 1978.

Jakubowski-Spector, P. Facilitating the growth of women through assertive training. *Counseling Psychologist,* 1973, *4,* 75-86.

Rathus, S. A. Principles and practices of assertive training: An eclectic overview. *Counseling Psychologist,* 1975, *5,* 9-20.

Module 7: Group process

An essential axiom of group theory is the distinction between member and class and the fact that a class cannot be a member of itself. The behavior of a group cannot be understood, for example, by the behavior of an individual within the group multiplied by its number of members. Rather, a group is not just quantitatively different from the individuals who comprise it but qualitatively different as well. For this reason certain things can be said about how individuals interact that may be helpful to nurses in the ICU, who, of course, comprise a group themselves.

The Johari Window (Luft, 1970) is one way to illustrate the relationships between individuals in a group. The four quadrants of the model are shown in Fig. A. The first quadrant represents those behaviors and motivations known both to the individual and to others. The second quadrant represents those behaviors which are apparent to others but not to the individual. The third quadrant is just the opposite and represents knowledge that the individual has that is not revealed to others. The fourth quadrant represents those things which, for the time being, are unknown both to the individual and to others.

These quadrants can represent several different changes that occur in group process. One principle is that a change in any one quadrant will affect the other three. An increase in quadrant one, for example, will correspondlingly decrease quadrant three; that is, a more open exchange with others will mean that less is hidden from them. Quadrant two, how-

	Known to self	Not known to self
Known to others	1 open	2 blind
Not known to others	3 hidden	4 unknown

FIG. A. (From *Group Processes: An Introduction to Group Dynamics* by Joseph Luft, by permission of Mayfield Publishing Company. Copyright (c) 1963, 1970 Joseph Luft.)

ever, will tend to change less readily because there usually are important psychological reasons for individuals to remain unconscious of certain things they say or do. Quadrant four will change even more slowly for many of these same reasons, although the unknown qualities it represents can be of great significance because of their potential for personal growth. The group and the individual will benefit most if quadrant one is enlarged and those in the group come to know more about themselves and others.

Another model of group communication is that of Bales (Jacobs, 1979), the categories of which are in reciprocal pairs, as illustrated in Table A. The usefulness of such a model is that it represents how you and others may tend to act in a group situation. Someone, for example, may have a number of suggestions for action (categories 4 and 6), or may simply agree (category 3) or disagree (category 10) with suggestions of others. What is important is that these roles remain open and flexible.

The functions within a group also have been characterized (Tubbs & Moss, 1974) and usually are regarded as one of two types, although neither alone is sufficient in itself to meet all the needs of the group. *Task functions* are those which help the group achieve its goals and include giving, and asking members for, suggestions and information as well as clarifying and summarizing information that already has been given. *Maintenance functions* are those which facilitate the working relationship of the group so that those tasks can be accomplished, such as encouraging members to contribute to the group and being responsive to their

Table A. Bales' model of group communication*

Positive (and mixed) actions	1. Seems friendly
	2. Dramatizes
	3. Agrees
Attempts answers	4. Gives suggestions
	5. Gives opinion
	6. Gives information
Questions	7. Asks for information
	8. Asks for opinion
	9. Asks for suggestions
Negative (and mixed) actions	10. Disagrees
	11. Shows tension
	12. Seems unfriendly

*From Personality and Interpersonal Behavior by Robert Freed Bales. Copyright © 1970 by Holt, Rinehart & Winston, Inc. Reprinted by permission of Holt, Rinehart & Winston.

comments. It is often difficult to perform both functions at the same time; however, they are necessary for the group to work constructively. For you to keep both in mind and take them on when necessary will help ensure that the group does so.

REFERENCES

Jacobs, M. K. Equilibrium theory applied to small nurse groups. *Advances in Nursing Science,* 1979, *1*(2), 23-39.

Luft, J. *Group process: An introduction to group dynamics* (2nd ed.). Palo Alto, Calif.: Mayfield, 1970.

Tubbs, S. L., & Moss, S. *Human communication: An interpersonal perspective.* New York: Random House, 1974.

Module 8: Conflict resolution

In a unit such as intensive care, where the work of the nurse is often critical, the resolution of conflict becomes important as well. By outlining the principles of conflict resolution, that often difficult process may be made somewhat easier.

An obvious first step in conflict resolution is the assumption that those involved be willing to change. Because the issues presumably are important enough to disagree over, attaining even this first step may be difficult. (Remember, if it were easy, there would be no conflict in the first place.) The particular issue, for example, may not always be clear. If it is defined too broadly and other, tangential items enter the conflict, there will be unnecessary discussion and debate. Often, too, an immediate reaction will be in response to personal feelings and not a contemplative consideration of the remarks of others. Especially if mutual distrust exists, an honest attempt for one person to understand the position of the other will be thwarted. Issues of power often make conflict resolution difficult. When factors are involved such as an aggressive sense of competition, the desire for a winner and a loser, or a certainty that there is only one way to do things (to the disregard of any other possible solution), little can be resolved.

Still, conflict can be conducive to growth and, in that sense, is healthy. In attempting to alleviate the tension or frustration that arises from individual differences over matters of importance, you are obliged to take some form of action. That action is what causes you to grow; it forces change and increases the rate at which it occurs.

Some conflict in the ICU may simply not be susceptible to change. Physicians, for example, may have to be absent from the unit, and although their absence may cause uncertainty about responsibility and priorities in emergencies, nothing can ensure their presence. However, there can be change—and growth. It may be better, for example, to reframe the problem (Watzlawick, Weakland, & Fisch, 1974), that is, to change, not its concrete reality, but the meaning attributed to it. Although the situation itself may have to remain unchanged, your perspective can still change.

Assuming that change is possible and there is a mutual desire to resolve the conflict, several other things can be done as well. Open dialogue should be encouraged. You should not only explain and clarify your own position but thoughtfully listen to the explanation of the other person, which will have the effect of clarifying the area of disagreement (and

agreement). It is possible, too, that understanding the real issue of conflict may allow the problem to be reframed and a new solution found. For
example, the absent physician may be a source of conflict that can be
resolved in other ways. Clear guidelines for emergencies and confidence
in one's own training and skill may help to alleviate some of the stress.

Another consideration should be the mechanics necessary for dialogue to take place successfully. Privacy and freedom from interruptions
are necessary and sufficient time to allow discussion of the problem con-
veniently. Although you need not compromise your objective, some sense
of flexibility will undoubtedly help to achieve it, if only because the most
long-lasting resolution will also be the most satisfying for all concerned.

In resolving conflict, next time keep the following points in mind:
- Is there a real desire on the other's part to resolve the conflict (and,
  you may ask yourself, on your own part as well)? If not, is there a
  way to make the other person more aware of the problem?
- Is there recognition that both persons can actually do something
  about the conflict; in other words, is it within your power to bring
  about some resolution?
- Although the resolution presumably will be acceptable to you, will
  it be accepted by the other person as well? Or will there have to be
  some compromise?
- Has the resolution been successful?

REFERENCE

Watzlawick, P., Weakland, J. H., & Fisch, R. *Change: Principles of problem formation and problem resolution.* New York: W. W. Norton, 1974.

Module 9: Crisis intervention

Patients in the ICU are often in crisis. It is important to recognize that the nurse who works there may sometimes be in crisis as well. In fact, at some point in their lives, almost everyone will experience periods of crisis.

When previously effective coping and adaptive mechanisms fail to resolve a particular problem, the resulting anxiety increases. This may often occur over days or weeks, distorting perception and rendering problem solving even more difficult, until a solution attainable by oneself is thought to be impossible. One is then in crisis. Crisis intervention (Aguilera & Messick, 1978) is the re-establishment of equilibrium between the problem and the resources that allow the individual to solve it—or, perhaps, to realize that the problem cannot be resolved. At the very least, effective crisis intervention should restore the person to the level of functioning that existed before the crisis. Adding to one's personal resources should also enhance the ability to cope with crises in the future.

Although the following steps outline crisis intervention with another individual, they may allow some better understanding when you, yourself, are in crisis.

- There should be an assessment of exactly what has precipitated the crisis. In other words, what has happened to make you believe that a crisis exists? One should ask as well how the event is perceived. What meaning does it have for the individual, and is it understood realistically? Often a distorted perception of the event occurs because of the anxiety that it elicits. Therefore, you should try to gain some understanding of the crisis and the acute discomfort that it is causing; for example, you should ask what is the worst part of the event and why did it become a crisis exactly when it did. Sometimes it helps to assist someone to express feelings which may not be immediately accessible to that individual alone, such as anger or grief. Such a catharsis can alleviate much of the pain that is felt.
- Because social support from those who care for and esteem the individual is especially important in times of crisis, you should recruit others who might be able to provide additional emotional support, for example, by listening to, or validating, the legitimacy of the emotions being felt.
- Past coping skills may not be effective. Are there any other behaviors that have been used before but have not yet been tried, or can new coping skills be suggested, for example, talking, crying, exer-

cising? By the learning of new skills when old ones have failed, growth can occur in crisis.

- There should be an awareness of the adaptive coping skills that have been used to reduce the anxiety of crisis successfully. By understanding exactly how a particular crisis has been resolved, other potential crises can be made less threatening.

REFERENCE

Aguilera, D. C., & Messick, J. M. *Crisis intervention: Theory and methodology.* (3rd ed.). St. Louis: C. V. Mosby, 1978.

Module 10: Problem solving

The existence of problems in the ICU may be obvious to you. How they began and how they persist in some instances but are resolved in others may be less clear.

Watzlawick, Weakland, and Fisch (1974) offer some important insights on the nature of change and the resolution of problems, which are reviewed here. Most obviously, a problem must actually *be* one if a solution is to be found for it. Pseudoproblems, or problems that are vaguely stated or imagined goals that are impractical and unreachable, can only compound the issue. It should be remembered, too, that some problems may have no solution and cannot, themselves, be changed. The way in which people regard those problems, however, *may* be changed.

Solutions also may be misdirected and so rendered ineffectual. A problem, for example, may be sustained because it is denied to be one. Although a solution is required, none is provided. Instead, people act as if the problem did not exist. Usually, if any difficulty is seen, it is with those who would point it out. They are seen as the problem, not the problem itself.

One is equally mistaken to attempt to find a solution for something that either is not susceptible to change or may not even exist. Instead of failing to take action when it is necessary, one attempts to take action when none is required. Both approaches to problem solving are similar and equally ineffectual. In one situation, where a problem exists, no one sees it; in the other situation, a solution is offered when none is needed. An example of the latter approach is the nurse who somehow may feel inadequate because certain goals cannot be reached. Instead of reassessing those possibly unrealistic or unattainable goals, however, the nurse is blamed for failing to meet them. In this case the solution is the problem, not the problem itself. The notion that things should (or can) be a certain way is the problem that requires change.

A final wrong attempt at problem solving is to take some action but at an inappropriate level. There are some situations, for example, for which solutions cannot be generated from their own context; instead, change has to come from an entirely different level. Failing to realize this only perpetuates the problem. Continuing to apply more of a particular solution when it is inappropriate in the first place is an example. Another is requiring more change than is necessary, for example, demanding a change in attitude when a change in behavior is sufficient.

Paradoxically, commonsense and logical attempts to solve a problem may fail. For this reason Watzlawick et al. suggest "reframing" as a means of problem resolution, in which the meaning attributed to the situation is changed (even though the situation itself may remain the same). Often, solutions fail because the assumption that a choice has to be made between two particular alternatives blinds one to other choices. The advantage of reframing is that, once a change in perspective occurs, it is usually difficult to regard the problem as it was originally, for example a puzzle that, once it has been solved and an answer provided, is no longer regarded as perplexing.

Reframing can be especially helpful in resolving those situations which demand a spontaneous response. Because spontaneity, by its very nature, cannot occur if expected, such situations may not lend themselves to commonsensible solutions. Falling asleep, for instance, by trying to do so may be more difficult than if no effort were made at all. The seemingly logical solution in this case is actually the problem. Paradoxically, the real solution (not to try so hard or even to stay awake) is regarded as the problem in the unreframed perspective.

Another approach to problem solving is provided by Claus and Bailey (1975). In this model a problem is regarded as a discrepancy between what should be and what is. It is important that both these situations be clearly understood. Goals should be sufficiently specific so that they can be used later to determine the effectiveness of the solution, and the problem should be perceived accurately enough to permit an appropriate response to it. It may possibly be solved in several different ways. Whatever alternatives are chosen, they must meet the criteria that have been set. Certain constraints, for instance, may limit the choices that can be made, and there may be other objectives that should be included in any solution. It is also important that the solution be evaluated. If it has not been effective, the systematic approach outlined in Claus and Bailey's model should provide an indication of where in the sequence difficulties first became evident.

REFERENCES

Bailey, J. T., & Claus, K. E. *Decision making in nursing: Tools for change.* St. Louis: C. V. Mosby, 1975.

Watzlawick, P., Weakland, J., & Fisch, R. *Change: Principles of problem formation and problem resolution.* New York: W. W. Norton, 1974.

Module 11: Death and dying

The dying patient is a source of stress to the nurse. This can be especially so in the ICU, where death is more frequent and the challenge to prevent it is more demanding.

As Glaser and-Strauss (1965) have indicated, the interaction between the dying patient and the nurse can be of several kinds: (1) the patient may not recognize his impending death, although the nurse does; (2) the patient suspects that he is dying and attempts to confirm that suspicion; (3) both nurse and patient understand that he is dying, although each pretends otherwise; or (4) both nurse and patient understand that he is dying and act on this awareness. Each of these contexts, of course, has an effect on the interactions between patient and nurse. Whether the patient should be told of his impending death and what is to be done if he knows, does not know, or only suspects that fact are problems with obvious implications for the nurse.

1. The problem of what Glaser and Strauss have called the "closed awareness context" is in maintaining it. If the patient is to be sustained in the hope of recovery, there should be no cues that would reveal his actual condition. Although such a context can usually be maintained, if only because the patient must depend on others for his assessment, it is often accomplished only with considerable stress for the nurse.

2. This stress increases when the patient does become suspicious of his true condition and seeks to elicit cues from the nurse. In not providing them, for instance, the nurse must deny the claim of the patient for more information while hoping at the same time that the patient will not deny the claim that the nurse makes on him not to provide it.

3. Another interaction between patient and nurse is that of mutual pretense. Both know that the patient is dying but pretend that he is not. Although such a context avoids a confrontation with the reality of death, it may be difficult to maintain, especially if the patient is deteriorating or is unwilling to confront death alone.

4. Open awareness is a context in which both patient and nurse are aware that the patient is dying, although when that death may occur is still unknown. Ironically, this shared knowledge permits other problems. Since the nurse is no longer obliged to maintain either ignorance or pretense about the patient's condition, both must now confront the reality of the patient's death and the difficulties it may cause.

The interaction between patient and nurse is largely determined by the behavior of the patient. The patient who, aware that he is dying, acts with composure and dignity and cooperates with the nurse is appreci-ated. This desire to have a poignant situation made less so also may be one reason why patient and nurse sometimes maintain the pretense of recovery or why the patient may not even want to know that he is dying.

Aside from these awareness contexts, Glaser and Strauss (1968) speak of the "trajectory of death." Although the assessment of whether a patient is dying and when it will occur is not always easy, that death can be described, at least, as certain or uncertain and at a known or unknown time. In the ICU the typical trajectory, or course, of the dying patient is usually certain and known, unless there can be some intervention. It is the satisfaction, in fact, of saving the dying patient that provides much of the motivation and challenge in the unit. For that reason patients whose course of dying is either lingering or terminal are less likely to be admit-ted there.

When a patient is expected to die can affect the behavior of the nurse, just as the way in which the patient dies. Because patients typically are not in the ICU for an extended period of time, there is less chance that their loss will have an adverse effect on the nurse, although there still can be a great sense of social loss, especially if the patient is young, thought to be talented, or even reminds the nurse of someone else.

Because in mourning the death of others people often lament for themselves as well, it may help for you to make yourself more aware of your own feelings about death. Epstein (1975) suggests several ways. How, for example, do you want other people to act when you die? How would you, yourself, want to be treated? Do you really believe that you are going to die? By answering questions such as these and better under-standing your own notions of death and its significance, the death of others can be more easily confronted.

REFERENCES

Epstein, C. *Nursing and the dying patient: Learning processes for interaction.* Reston, Va.: Reston, 1975.

Glaser, B. G., & Strauss, A. L. *Awareness of dying.* New York: Macmillan, 1965.

Glaser, B. G., & Strauss, A. L. *Time for dying.* New York: Macmillan, 1968.

Module 12: Ethics

The ethical issues confronted in the ICU can be considerably stressful. The care of patients, for which the nurse is largely responsible, at times presents profound ethical dilemmas regarding patient suffering and autonomy, the withholding or termination of treatment, and the definiton of death. Yet, the nurse often has little formal input in the resolution of these issues.

Implicit in the relationship between patient and physician (and the nurse) is that the patient can be helped. By this therapeutic agreement the patient will follow the physician's recommendations, as long as they are in keeping with the patient's own values and goals. The physician will do everything possible to benefit the patient and will abstain from anything that would be harmful or useless to him, for example, interventions for profit or education, although, of course, informed patients could allow themselves to be involved in medical research.

Proper goals, however, are not always clear and may be different for the patient and physician. The same ability that permits medicine to save the lives of the critically ill also allows it to prolong the dying of those who cannot be healed. Some patients, however, may not want to live if severely disabled physically or mentally. This means that aggressive treatment until the patient dies may not always be justified. Not only may continued treatment in the ICU be inappropriate when it is without benefit to the patient, but its continuation can result in prolonging the suffering of the patient, his family, and the medical and nursing staff, as well as increasing the immense costs of ICU service. Discontinuing treatment, however, raises other questions, for example, the loss of a patient who otherwise might have been saved.

If there is disagreement over patient care, it would seem that, ethically, the goals of the patient should be respected and have priority over those of the physician. If the patient is incompetent, or has left no written directions for his care (e.g., a living will), or does not want to participate in it, the patient's family should be involved in any decision about the continuation of treatment. But, again, there are questions. The incompetent patient or the distressed family may not be able, or have the knowledge, to make the necessary critical decisions, in which case the physician (or even a court of law) must do so in the best interests of the patient.

Whether or not the patient can continue to benefit from intensive care is a difficult prognosis, nor is it always possible to determine who should make that decision. The clinical judgment which is used, however, should be clearly outlined so that the medical and nursing staff, as well as the patient and his family, know exactly why a particular intervention has been chosen, where it may lead, and its proper limits.

This means that there should be agreement, or certainly discussion, on a number of ethical issues—whether, for instance, a patient should be told of his impending death. It is possible that the patient really does not want to know that he is dying or that such knowledge would be disruptive to the unit. It may be thought that the patient will cooperate more readily with the staff if there is hope for recovery. The patient's family also may find it easier to confront someone who is ignorant of his death, especially if it is suspected that the knowledge cannot be accepted with composure.

Yet, there are obvious ethical considerations in such a decision. One may ask whether anyone should, by withholding information, deny a dying person the right to know of an imminent death and to make personal arrangements for it. Because the burden of dealing with the unaware patient falls most persistently on the nurse, maintaining that ignorance can be particularly stressful.

The termination of therapeutic efforts is another dilemma. Although there is an obligation to provide care that is beneficial and conducive to the patient's recovery, when such care is no longer possible, that responsibility must necessarily change. The form that it takes, however, may not always be certain, for example, whether ordinary or extraordinary measures should be used to keep the patient alive or whether some steps should be taken to promote the downward trajectory of his death. When that death actually occurs and how it is to be defined are other questions which must be posed.

How one answers these professional questions depends, in turn, on a personal ethic for which answers may be elusive but which can gain definition from the work setting.

SUGGESTED READINGS

Davis, A. J. Ethic rounds with intensive care nurses. *Nursing Clinics of North America,* 1979, *14,* 45-55.
Davis, A. J., & Aroskar, M. A. *Ethical dilemmas in nursing practice.* New York: Appleton-Century-Crofts, 1978.

Module 13: Management of the unit

Ironically, this module on the management of the unit as a source of stress for the ICU nurse is short, even though that particular source of stress is equally great. The reason for this disparity between the significance of the stressor and the attention paid to it is that many administrative decisions which relate to the management of the unit, such as staffing and admissions, are not immediately subject to the control of the nurse.

The nurse can, and should, respond to those decisions, however. In doing so, several things should be kept in mind. One is that problems in the unit are not exclusively those of the administration or the staff for one or the other to solve alone; they should be corrected by both, if possible. Such collaboration, rather than confrontation, should better remedy those problems which are subject to change. It is important to remember, too, that some problems may not be. The nurse may have to cope with them and the decisions made affecting them.

Unit administration also can benefit from understanding what is professionally satisfying to the nurses who work there. Although studies on job satisfaction (Cronin-Stubbs, 1977; Everly & Falcione, 1976; Longest, 1974; Slavitt, Stamps, Piedmont, & Haase, 1978; Slocum, Susman, & Sheridan, 1972; Ullrich, 1978) are characterized by the diversity of their conclusions, certain aspects of work, such as self-actualization, achievement, and autonomy, are obviously important factors in work satisfaction. The administration may not always be aware of this, although it should be. A study by Benson and White (1972), for instance, indicated that patient care, although ranked first or second in importance by practicing nurses, was ranked fifteenth (of sixteen factors) by administrative nurses. Yet, if the proper management of the unit is to be agreed on by administration and staff, both must understand one another.

REFERENCES

Benson, D. A. & White, H. C. Satisfaction of job factors for registered nurses. *Journal of Nursing Administration,* 1972, 2(6), 55-63.

Cronin-Stubbs, D. Job satisfaction and dissatisfaction among new graduate staff nurses. *Journal of Nursing Administration,* 1977, 7(10), 44-49.

Everly, G. S., II, & Falcione, R. L. Perceived dimensions of job satisfaction for staff registered nurses. *Nursing Research,* 1976, 25, 346-348.

Longest, B. B. Job satisfaction for registered nurses in the hospital setting. *Journal of Nursing Administration,* 1974, 4(3), 46-52.

Slavitt, D. B., Stamps, P. L., Piedmont, E. B., & Haase, A. M. B. Nurses' satisfaction with their work situation. *Nursing Research,* 1978, 27, 114-120.

Slocum, J. W., Jr., Susman, G. I., & Sheridan, J. E. An analysis of need satisfaction and job performance among professional and paraprofessional hospital personnel. *Nursing Research,* 1972, *21,* 338-342.

Ullrich, R. A. Herzberg revisited: Factors in job dissatisfaction. *Journal of Nursing Administration,* 1978, 8(10), 19-24.

Module 14: Inadequate knowledge and skills

It is the strong professional and technical emphasis of the ICU that allows procedures there to be in the vanguard of medical and nursing practice. At the same time, however, the competence of the nurse, as well as its broad knowledge base, can be sources of considerable stress to the nurse. Highly complex and specialized equipment can malfunction, and patients can require varied treatments and regimens. Because procedures that are potentially life saving become equally life threatening when mistakes are made, the operation of equipment and correct patient assessment and intervention are even more critical in the ICU.

Sufficient training for work in the ICU, however, may not have been acquired in school, and even with a period of orientation, the new nurse on the unit may be confronted with situations which are largely unfamiliar and even somewhat intimidating, especially if that orientation was thought to have been too brief or if expectations of the nurse are made too soon.

Yet, aside from in-service education, the nurse can do several things to increase individual knowledge and skills and so reduce the stress that occurs when they are thought to be inadequate. Simply asking another person may be the easiest way to have questions answered about equipment or particular procedures in the ICU that are unfamiliar. The nurse also can take advantage of continuing education courses in those areas for which there is personal accountability or interest. Reading the professional literature is another way to increase one's knowledge. Journals such as *Critical Care Quarterly, Critical Care Update, Heart and Lung,* and *Critical Care Medicine* are especially helpful and could be made available at work. Even articles tacked to a bulletin board can be an effective way to share new information.

These suggestions are easy and obvious enough. What may be more difficult is to distinguish between needs which are felt and those which are real. The nurse, for example, may feel uneasy about a particular skill that, when it has been demonstrated, is found to be perfectly adequate. (Just the opposite could also be the case.) This is why it is important that the nurse be aware of the difference between what, personally, may be thought sufficient (or insufficient) and what actually is so. If those two perceptions are the same, the stress caused by situations that demand new knowledge and skills will lessen as quickly as those experiences are encountered and so made familiar.

Because of the nurse's education and training and the realization that any deficiency in that preparation can be remedied by staff development, peer support, or one's self-directed learning, inadequate knowledge and skills are among the least stressful aspects of ICU nursing. In a unit where nursing intervention is critical, this is as it should be. More important than devising ways to correct those deficiencies is a clear recognition of what they are and whether they are real or imagined.

Module 15: Physical work environment

The physical environment of the ICU, itself, can be a source of stress for the nurse who works there. Certainly, it can be for the patient. "Intensive care syndrome" has been described as a psychiatric condition affecting patients in the ICU that is related to the particular environment of the unit (Kornfeld, 1971; McKegney, 1966). Antiseptic, often windowless, and filled with unfamiliar and complex equipment, the ICU setting assails the new patient with strange, even ominous, sights and sounds. Together with interrupted sleep, restrained movement, and sensory deprivation, it is not surprising that such stimuli can occasionally lead to disorientation and a loss of psychological equilibrium.

For the nurse who works in the ICU, its environment has become familiar and routine. Still, the setting can be a source of stress, if only because the unit has been designed to meet the physiological needs of the patient, not the psychological needs of the nurse. If the two conflict, those of the patient usually must have priority. Consequently, temperature comfortable for the patient may be too warm (or too cool) for the nurse. Space, too, is often limited, both because of the need for equipment in proximity to the patient and because the unit itself probably has been created from space that already existed in the hospital and so may not be as effectively used as it could be. In an emergency, crowding may occur, although ironically the nurse may feel isolated and alone at other times. The highly technical and sophisticated equipment, which can take up so much room, can be an obvious source of stress when it malfunctions. Not only can it be surprisingly noisy (Bentley, Murphy, & Dudley, 1977; Turner, King, & Craddock, 1975), but it is also impossible for the nurse to adjust to such noise, since warning signals and signs of malfunction must constantly be monitored.

Patients, too, must be watched, with the result that nurses in the ICU have little privacy. The need for time and space away from the unit for the nurse to relax and find some temporary respite is especially important in the ICU. Removing oneself from the source of stress, of course, is not as satisfactory a solution as eliminating the stressors themselves. The physical work environment of the ICU, however, may not be susceptible to change or only to such change as required by the patients, and even these requirement (e.g., in lighting and temperature) may vary among individuals. Fortunately, the environment is not regarded as a major source of stress; certainly, it is not as stressful as interpersonal relationships or patient care. What cannot be remedied, however, should at least be recognized.

REFERENCES

Bentley, S., Murphy, F., & Dudley, H. Perceived noise in surgical wards and an intensive care area: An objective analysis. *British Medical Journal,* 1977, 2, 1503-1506.

Kornfeld, D. S. Psychiatric problems of an intensive care unit. *Medical Clinics of North America,* 1971, 55, 1353-1363.

McKegney, F. P. The intensive care syndrome: The definition, treatment and prevention of a new "disease of medical progress." *Connecticut Medicine,* 1966, 30, 633-636.

Turner, A. G., King, C. H. & Craddock, J. G. Measuring and reducing noise. *Hospitals,* 1975, 49(15), 85-86; 88; 90.

Index